KT-366-244

REFRESHER COURSES FOR
METHODIST LOCAL PREACHERS

Number 1 New Series

JOHN A. NEWTON

The Fruit of the Spirit in the Lives of Great Christians

London EPWORTH PRESS

© *John A. Newton 1979*
First published 1979
by Epworth Press
All rights reserved

No part of this publication
may be reproduced, stored in a
retrieval system, or
transmitted, in any form or by
any means, electronic, mechanical,
photocopying, recording or
otherwise, without the prior
permission of Epworth Press

7162 0328 6

Enquiries should be addressed to
The Methodist Publishing House
Wellington Road
Wimbledon
London SW19 8EU
Printed in Great Britain by
The Garden City Press Limited,
Letchworth, Hertfordshire SG6 1JS

Contents

Preface   7

Introduction   9

CHAPTER ONE
The Fruit of the Spirit is Love
Mother Teresa of Calcutta   13

CHAPTER TWO
The Fruit of the Spirit is Joy
St Francis of Assisi   23

CHAPTER THREE
The Fruit of the Spirit is Peace
George Fox   34

CHAPTER FOUR
The Fruit of the Spirit is Patience
Dora Greenwell   43

CHAPTER FIVE
The Fruit of the Spirit is Gentleness
Edward King   52

CHAPTER SIX
The Fruit of the Spirit is Self-control
Richard Baxter   60

Preface

These short studies are a revised and expanded version of material brought together to form a six-week Lenten Course. The course was first given at Wotton-under-Edge, Gloucestershire, for the churches of the Christian Council there. It was repeated, in a revised form, for the Christians of the Ecumenical Parish of St Alban's, Westbury Park, Bristol.

I am grateful to those who first heard the talks for the comments and suggestions made in response to them. I have tried to bear these in mind in preparing the studies for publication. I should also like to express my gratitude to my secretary, Mrs Brenda Bridges, for her patience and accuracy in reducing my untidy manuscript to an immaculate typescript. I am also much indebted to the Reverend John Stacey of the Methodist Publishing House for urging me, with kind persistence, to publish them in the new series of Refresher Courses for Local Preachers of the Methodist Church which he has planned. He encourages me to hope that this little book may be serviceable to that end, and may even, perhaps, be of interest to a wider readership. If it helps some to explore the fullness of Christian life and character, in the pages of the New Testament and in the lives of some of the most ardent followers of Christ, I shall be satisfied.

Kingsway Hall, London   JOHN A. NEWTON

But the harvest of the Spirit is love, joy, peace, patience, kindness, goodness, fidelity, gentleness and self-control.

Galatians 5:22 *New English Bible*

Introduction

In Galatians 5:22 the Greek word for 'Fruit of the Spirit' is *karpos*. It is in the singular, as if to stress that all the various Christian graces find their unity in the Spirit-filled life of the believer. We shall look at some of the grace-gifts of the Spirit separately, holding them up to the light, like the facets of a diamond, one by one. Yet they form one single jewel, for they all come from the one Lord Jesus, and are all aspects of the one Christ-like character.

Looked at from another angle, the unity of the fruit of the Spirit is transparent in the way the Christian graces cohere and reinforce each other. If you are kind and patient and loving, you will know joy and peace. If you exercise self-control, that gift will show itself in gentleness and fidelity. The fruits of the Spirit are many; yet the fruit of the Spirit is one, ultimately, because it comes from the work of Christ within us.

There have always been Protestants who have been uneasy at turning the searchlight of devotion on the saints. To praise and honour the great athletes of the Spirit has seemed to them to detract from the glory of their Master. It is hard to understand why, for it is precisely Christ who is being honoured in his saints. As Gerard Manley Hopkins expresses the truth in his incomparable 'As Kingfishers catch fire . . .'

. . . the just man justices;
Keeps grace; that keeps all his goings graces,
Acts in God's eye what in God's eye he is—
Christ—for Christ plays in ten thousand places,
Lovely in limbs, and lovely in eyes not his
To the Father through the features of men's faces.

Yet, although all the varied fruits of the Spirit derive from the one Christ, and find their unity in Him, the lives of his saints highlight particular gifts. A sinner, as the old Puritans used to say, may have a 'darling sin', like a Delilah in his bosom. In an opposite, though analogous way, a saint may reveal in his life a special and peculiar grace. This grace may colour his whole character, and impart a characteristic flavour to his living, like the bouquet of a fine rare wine. It is for this reason that I have singled out the dominant note in the lives of six saints: love, in Mother Teresa of Calcutta; joy, in St Francis; peace, in George Fox; patience, in Dora Greenwell; gentleness, in Edward King; and self-control, in Richard Baxter.

Before we turn to our six saints, there is one further word to say. When we talk about the *fruit* of the Spirit in human lives, we are reminded that the sovereign test of Christian character and genuineness is the test of fruits; 'By their fruits you shall know them.' It is not said, 'By their visions, ecstasies, revelations, spectacular charismata;' but by their *fruits*. I never cease to be astonished that, in the midst of a tumultuous movement of religious revival, John Wesley could write such sober and searching words as these:

Another ground of these, and a thousand mistakes, is, the not considering deeply that love is the highest gift of

God—humble, gentle, patient love; that all visions, revelations, manifestations whatever, are little things com-
pared to love; and that all the gifts above mentioned are
either the same with or infinitely inferior to it . . . the
heaven of heavens is love. There is nothing higher in
religion—there is in effect, nothing else . . . And when
you are asking others 'have you received this or that
blessing?' if you mean anything but more love, you mean
wrong.[1]

Wesley's words on the centrality of love in the Christian life and character lead us appropriately to Mother
Teresa of Calcutta who has said: 'Love is a fruit that is
in season at all times, and within reach of every hand.
Anyone may gather it and no limit is set.'[2]

[1] John Wesley, *A Plain Account of Christian Perfection,* Epworth Press
(1952), p. 90
[2] Quoted in M. Muggeridge, *Something Beautiful for God*, Collins
Fontana (1972), p. 65

CHAPTER ONE

The Fruit of the Spirit is Love

Mother Teresa of Calcutta

The biblical meaning of love

When I was a Minister in Stockton-on-Tees, I soon encountered the extraordinary range and quality of its open-air market, one of the largest in England. There were the usual stalls selling flowers, fruit and vegetables, meat and fish. There were stalls with a profusion of cloth, woollens and dress-lengths from the West Riding. There were the more ephemeral, sometimes fly-by-night, here-today-and-gone-tomorrow stalls of the cheapjacks, never offering less than 'sensational bargains'. One day, passing through the market, I was arrested by the sight of a man on one of these stalls selling metal polish. He was not only singing the praises of his polish, with all the usual superlatives; he was also demonstrating its power. Rusty car hub-discs, blackened Victorian pennies, discoloured pots and pans were restored before our eyes to a shining, dazzling newness—with the aid of a lick of polish, a damp cloth and some elbow-grease. It was so impressive that I bought a tin on the spot, and afterwards regretted that I had not bought half a dozen.

If only we had a similarly powerful technique to remove the layers of misuse and distortion which, in common speech, so often deform the great words of faith. 'Love' is a prime example. Has any word in the language been more cheapened and prostituted? It takes a powerful flash of light, like the life of a modern saint, to illuminate for us what the biblical writers mean by *chesed* in the Hebrew or *agapē* in the Greek.

First of all, love comes from God. This is 'the love that moves the sun and the other stars'. It is strong, consistent, loyal, unbreakable. It is, in the Old Testament, often referred to as covenant-love, as an expression of God's loyalty to his loving purpose for Israel, and, through Israel, for all mankind. It has at its heart an utter faithfulness, like the deep, passionate love of a mother for her child, which may give us a glimpse of what God's love is like. Kipling's words may be well-worn, but they still have a haunting, elemental simplicity:

> If I were drowned in the deepest sea,
> O mother of mine, O mother of mine,
> I know whose love would come down to me,
> O mother of mine, O mother of mine.

Johann Jakob Schultz's great hymn of thanksgiving contains one of the few references in Christian hymnology to mother-love as a reflex of the divine affection:

> As with a mother's tender hand,
> He leads His own, His chosen band;
> To God all praise and glory.[1]

It is this quality of intense, passionate commitment which we associate with a mother's love. If her child is seriously ill, her own need of sleep will drop dramatically to zero, as she watches by the bedside. If the child dies, then—as has been said—no true woman

[1] *Methodist Hymn Book,* 415, v. 3

14

ever really gets over the death of her child. But where a mother's love is deep, but narrow, for her own, God's love is wide as the world, for every single human being.

God is not on the side of the big battalions. If he has favourites, they are the poor and downtrodden. So the message comes to the Israelites, freed from the Egyptian slave-labour camps, 'It was not because you were more numerous than any other nation that the Lord cared for you and chose you . . . It was because the Lord loved you'.[2] God helps those who help themselves? Well, yes; but the countervailing truth is that God helps those who cannot help themselves.

Moreover, his love persists even when those whom he loves prove to be faithless, weak and sinful. As the word of the Lord came to Hosea, 'Go again, and love a woman loved by another man, an adultress, and love her as I the Lord love the Israelites'.[3]

The supreme place where we see God's faithful, covenant-love for the loveless, is in Jesus. God's love gives itself to all mankind unreservedly. 'God loved the world so much that he gave his only Son, that everyone who has faith in him may not die but have eternal life.'[4] Of this golden text, the great Puritan scholar, Richard Baxter (1615–1691) wrote: 'If it had said, "God so loved Richard Baxter", then I should have thought it must mean some other Richard Baxter; but when it says "God so loved the world" I know that that includes all the Richard Baxters that ever shall be.'

The sign of the presence of God's love in our hearts

[2] Deuteronomy 7:7, 8
[3] Hosea 3:1
[4] John 3:16

is that we love others. It is again the test of fruits. This is the gold standard, as far as Christian ethics is concerned. 'We love, because He loved us first. But if a man says "I love God" while hating his brother, he is a liar. If he does not love the brother whom he has seen, it cannot be that he loves God whom he has not seen.'[5]

Mother Teresa of Calcutta

We turn now to look at the love of Jesus as that is embodied and enfleshed in the life of Mother Teresa, a life which has been aptly styled, *Something Beautiful for God*.

Malcolm Muggeridge's title echoes, of course, the Gospel account of Jesus and the penitent harlot, who broke the box of precious ointment of spikenard over his feet. Of the women's action Jesus exclaimed: 'She has done a beautiful thing to me.'[6] It was 'beautiful' (*kalos* in the Greek, implying attractive as well as morally praiseworthy), because it was a prodigal, lavish, sacrificial outpouring of love and self-giving at the feet of Christ. 'She has anointed my body for the burying.'[7] Mysteriously, her act is linked to his Passion, for on Calvary too there was, beyond all comparison, a great, prodigal outpouring of love and self-giving. Charles Wesley, in his hymn 'Depth of mercy! Can there be' refers to this incident, and more especially to the carping criticism of the woman's action which came from the scribes: 'Why this waste?' But Wesley applies the criticism, not to the unnamed

[5] 1 John 4:19, 20
[6] Mark 14:6
[7] Mark 14:8

woman of the Gospel, but to Christ Crucified, whose love lies bleeding for the whole world:

> Whence to me this waste of love?
> Ask my Advocate above!
> See the cause in Jesu's face,
> Now before the throne of grace.[8]

As we turn to Mother Teresa, it is well to remember that there were not lacking critics who, when she gave up her teaching for a ministry to the poorest of the poor, interposed the same question: 'Why this waste?'

By birth a humble peasant woman, Mother Teresa was born in Yugoslavia, of Albanian parents. She taught for some years in Loreto Convent School for Girls in Calcutta, and then heard Christ's call to leave the quiet, happy, absorbing life of the school and go into the slums. She knew her call was to live and serve among the destitute. She saw the change not as any kind of flamboyant or dramatic gesture, but as a simple act of obedience to Christ. With her peasant background, she is no vague idealist, but of the earth, earthy. Malcolm Muggeridge can write of her that, 'Without the special grace vouchsafed her, she might have been a rather hard, and even grasping, person. God has turned these qualities to his own ends. I never met anyone less sentimental, less scatty, more down-to-earth.'[9]

She and her Sisters are identified with the poor, and share their life. 'They eat the same food, wear the same clothes, possess as little, are not permitted to

---

[8] *Methodist Hymn Book* 358, v. 3
[9] M. Muggeridge, *Something Beautiful for God*, p. 18

have a fan or any other mitigations of life in Bengal's sweltering heat.'[10] It is typical of Mother Teresa's realism, however, that although her Sisters eat the same kind of food as the poor, they have more of it. She came to see that her Sisters, unlike the poor beggars, would have to sustain a full day's work on the food they ate. Fed on a starvation diet, they would soon have succumbed to malnutrition and tuberculosis and would have been in no condition to help the poor.

What does Mother Teresa's life teach us about the grace of Christian love? First, by the quality of her life and ministry, she embodies that love of God for whom every single person is of infinite value, every last, least, lowest human being, no matter how wretched. She has taken abandoned babies out of dustbins, and treasured and loved them into life. As gold dust to a miser, to this woman every small scrap of humanity is precious. Why? Because she takes seriously her Lord's words that 'Inasmuch as you did to one of the least of these my brothers, you did it to me'.[11] So she looks upon every beggar left to die in the streets as Christ himself.

Again, Mother Teresa is a window on to the world of Christian love because of her gospel sense of priorities. In John Wesley's phrase, she is concerned to go not only to those who need her, but to those who need her most. It has been said that the Christian minister should have a nose for trouble, an instinct for tragedy; not in any lugubrious sense, but so that he may make an instant pastoral response. In a similar way, Malcolm Muggeridge can speak of Mother

[10] Ibid., p. 16
[11] Matthew 25:40

18

Teresa's 'Geography of compassion'. He writes of how 'She heard that in Venezuela there are abandoned poor; so off the Sisters go there, and a house is set up. Then that in Rome . . . there are derelicts, as in Calcutta. Or again, that in Australia the aboriginals and half-castes need love and care. In each case, wherever it may be, the call is heard and answered.'[12]

Moreover, for Mother Teresa service to the poor is not enough. The corporal works of mercy are of course central to her ministry. But it has been said—and Mother Teresa of all people would understand the saying—that unless you love the poor they may hate you for the very bread you give them. For Mother Teresa 'The poor . . . deserve not just service and dedication, but also the joy that belongs to human love'.[13] Their greatest need of all is to be wanted, valued, cared for, loved. And if they must die, then she will move heaven and earth to let them die 'within sight of a loving face'.

There is also in this woman a good deal of the audacious hopefulness of Christian love. Hers is a faith that works by love and has great expectations. Like William Carey, another great apostolic figure in the history of Indian Christianity, she both attempts great things for God, and expects great things from God. Hers is the love that hopes all things and endures all things. So she pitches the requirements of her Order at what might seem , in the Indian context, an impossibly high level—and evokes an extraordinary response. Malcolm Muggeridge expresses his own amazement:

[12] M. Muggeridge, op. cit., p. 60
[13] Ibid., p. 49

> I should never have believed it possible, knowing India as I do over a number of years, to induce Indian girls of good family to tend outcasts and untouchables brought in from Calcutta streets. Yet this, precisely, is the very first task that Mother Teresa gives them to do when they come to her as postulants. They do it, not just in obedience, but cheerfully and ardently, and gather round her in ever greater numbers for the privilege of doing it.[14]

Finally, Mother Teresa's work of love is rooted in her faith in Christ. One of her favourite sayings is, 'No longer I, but Christ lives in me'. She is utterly Christ-centred, and shows her belief, in all she does, that, 'We love, because He first loved us'. She avows that she could not get through a single day of her work without the regular encounter with Christ in the mass. 'In Holy Communion,' she says, 'we have Christ under the appearance of bread. In our work we find him under the appearance of flesh and blood. It is the same Christ.'[15]

There is a whole mystical and sacramental theology implicit in those deceptively simple words. They knit together faith and works, devotion and discipleship, the active and passive elements in the Christian life.

Mother Teresa is not only a revelation of the power of Christian love in the modern world. She also poses uncomfortable questions for contemporary church life. First, are our priorities of mission and caring anywhere near right? We know we are called to minister, as we have opportunity, to all men; but what of the peculiar claim made upon us by 'those who need us most'? They are not the untouchables and dying street beggars of Calcutta, but they are, among others,

14 Ibid., p. 52
15 Ibid., p. 74

the bedrock poor, the drop-outs, alcoholics, homeless, mentally ill, prisoners, the despairing and the suicidal. How often do their names and needs come before us in our pious 'Conversations on the work of God'?

Again, Mother Teresa is a sign pointing unmistakably to the truth that those who would serve others in Christ's name, must drink deeply of the means of grace. Only if we abide in his love, can we bear much fruit. That great Methodist prophet, the late Daniel ('D. T.') Niles, was once walking through the countryside in his native Sri Lanka, with his small son by his side. They came across an open-air wrestling booth, and the child gazed open-mouthed at the contestants, grunting and heaving away in the ring. He was even more impressed when, at the end of a bout, they retired to their corners for food. As he watched them put away great quantities of meat and rice and fruit, the little boy whispered to his father in an awed voice, 'Daddy, if I ate as much as that, it would kill me.' 'Yes,' his father agreed, 'it would; but you're not a wrestler.'

Are we? If we are genuinely wrestling with human need, seeking to overcome evil with good, in the ministries of Christian love, we shall need to eat hearty and drink deep at the banquet of God's grace in Jesus.

SUGGESTED FURTHER READING
On the nature of Christian Love:
A. Nygren, *Agape and Eros,* 2 vols. in 3 (1932–39)
M. C. D'Arcy, *The Mind and Heart of Love* (1945)
J. Burnaby, *Amor Dei*: *a study of the religion of St Augustine* (1938)

W. H. Vanstone, *Love's Endeavour, Love's Expense* (1977)

On Mother Teresa:
E. Le Joly, *We do it for Jesus* (1977)

REFRESHER COURSE EXERCISE
Plan a sermon based on one of the following texts:
Deut. 7:7–8a; Hos. 3:1; 1 John 4: 19–20, illustrating,
where possible, from the life and work of Mother
Teresa.

CHAPTER TWO

The Fruit of the Spirit is Joy

St Francis of Assisi

The biblical meaning of joy

In the Old Testament, joy is the frank accompaniment of material blessings: plenty of corn, wine, oil, flocks, herds, sons and daughters. Such prosperity brings joy not only for its own sake, but because it is a pretty clear indicator that God favours the recipient. As the sixteenth-century translation of Genesis has it: 'The Lord was with Joseph, and he was a lucky fellow.'

The Book of Job, however, puts a massive question mark against any neat equation of material blessings with the favour of God. It also vehemently contests the view that, when sorrows and sufferings fall thick upon a man, they denote God's judgement and displeasure. Yet even in Job, it is the prosperous sheikh –both before the calamity, and afterwards, with his fortunes restored—who knows joy. In the midst of the dire distress, Job knows only sorrow and heart-searching. Faith and hope may break through, magnificently and against all the odds, but not joy. 'Weeping may tarry for the night, but joy cometh in the morning.'[1] Trouble and joy are mutually exclusive, oil and water, and it would seem, on this reckoning, foolish to think otherwise.

In the New Testament, however, we come to a deeper strand of the biblical meaning of joy. As so

[1] Psalm 30:5 (R.V.)

often in the deepest mysteries of human life, we find an intermingling of opposite emotions and experiences: an enormous enhancement of life in the midst of danger and death; love and hate intertwined in a complex relation between two persons; and joy and sorrow woven fine. George Matheson's well-known hymn, 'O love that wilt not let me go', has suffered emasculation in its crucial third verse. In its published form it reads:

> O joy that seekest me through pain,
> I cannot close my heart to Thee:
> I trace the rainbow through the rain
> And feel the promise is not vain,
> That morn shall tearless be.[2]

What Matheson actually wrote, having gone blind and been jilted by his fiancée, was not the consolatory 'I *trace* the rainbow through the rain', but the exultant 'I *climb* the rainbow through the rain'. There is all the difference here between the typical Old Testament understanding of joy and that which stamps its impress on the New.[3]

In the New Testament itself, there are numerous examples of this concatenation of joy and sorrow. Take the incident in Acts 5, where Peter and John, having healed the crippled beggar at the Temple gate, have been arrested, warned not to preach in the name of Jesus any more, and then arrested for a second,

---

[2] *Methodist Hymn Book*, 448, v. 3.

[3] There are, of course, magnificent anticipations of the New Testament understanding under the Old Covenant—see, for example, Habakkuk 3:17, 18; and compare William Cowper's 'Sometimes a light surprises' (*Methodist Hymn Book,* No. 527) written in his lifeblood by a Christian who had to endure excruciating bouts of mental illness bordering on madness.

identical offence. The Sanhedrin, 'sent for the apostles, and had them flogged; then they ordered them to give up speaking in the name of Jesus, and discharged them. So the apostles went out from the Council *rejoicing* that they had been found worthy to suffer indignity for the sake of the Name,'[4] James counsels his fellow-Christians, 'My brothers, count it all *joy* when you have to face trials of many kinds'.[5] Peter strikes the same note in his first epistle: 'My dear friends, do not be bewildered by the fiery ordeal that is upon you as though it were something extraordinary. It gives you a share in Christ's sufferings, and that is cause for *joy*.'[6]

For these first Christians, joy was found in the midst of pain and at the heart of sorrow. It was a joy that surmounted all the slings and arrows of outrageous fortune. They were not exempt from trials. Quite the reverse; their faith brought added ills upon them, and compounded the tale of their sufferings. But they had a medicine which could extract the poison from the hurt. They had lighted upon some strange alchemy that could turn it all to gold. They learned this secret at the foot of Christ's cross—at the mouth of his tomb. Their joy, irrefragable as it seemed, was rooted in their experience of Christ crucified and risen. It was confirmed and deepened as they suffered in the name and for the sake of Christ. They were not Spartans or Stoics, but they found they could rejoice, in the fellowship of his sufferings and the power of his resurrection. So they accepted all that life laid upon them, and offered it to God, in the conviction that he could and

[4] Acts 5:40, 41
[5] James 1:2
[6] 1 Peter 4:12, 13

25

would use the sacrifice in his everlasting purpose of overcoming evil with good, and summing up all things in Christ. It is a joy of this New Testament quality that we see in the life of Francesco Bernardone, St Francis of Assisi.

St Francis of Assisi (1182–1226)

Much has been written about St Francis in our century, not least in 1976, the 750th anniversary of his death, which called forth a great spate of books and articles from printing presses all over the world. Much of the writing, naturally enough, came from the pens of Christians; but by no means all. St Francis is one of those towering figures in the Christian story who appeal to unbelievers almost as much as to believers. Norman MacCaig, for instance, is no professing Christian, but in his poem 'Assisi' he comes very near to the heart of St Francis, and to the mind of Christ.

ASSISI

The dwarf with his hands on backwards
sat, slumped like a half-filled sack
on tiny twisted legs from which
sawdust might run,
outside the three tiers of churches built
in honour of St Francis, brother
of the poor, talker with birds, over whom
he had the advantage
of not being dead yet.

A priest explained
how clever it was of Giotto
to make his frescoes tell stories
that would reveal to the illiterate the goodness

of God and the suffering
of His Son. I understood
the explanation and
the cleverness.

A rush of tourists, clucking contentedly,
fluttered after him as he scattered
the grain of the Word. It was they who had passed
the ruined temple outside, whose eyes
wept pus, whose back was higher
than his head, whose lopsided mouth
said Grazie in a voice as sweet
as a child's when she speaks to her mother
or a bird's when it spoke
to St Francis.[7]

St Francis was born Francesco Bernadone, the son
of a wealthy cloth merchant of North Italy, one of the
most advanced regions—culturally and economi-
cally—in medieval Europe. Until he reached twenty-
one, he led the typically gay and careless life of a
young man of the rising, commercial middle class.
Then illness led to a deepened seriousness, a profound conversion, and the resolve to devote himself to
prayer and the service of the poor. It is striking but
perhaps not so strange, that the call to apostolic poverty has been so often heard against a background of
wealth and ease. One can understand the reaction
if one takes the point of Chesterton's counter-
aphorism: 'Nothing fails like success.' To have every
basic material want satisfied, and the money to satiate
the luxurious appetites as well, can so easily lead to
blasé indifference: so what? is this really all there is to
life? Again, St Francis' call reminds us how often God

[7] Taken from *Surroundings* published by The Hogarth Press in 1966.

speaks decisively to a man who has been stopped in his tracks by illness and made to take time out of his normal life. That period of enforced leisure may breed what Wordsworth calls a 'wise passiveness'; and through self-examination and insight, a man's whole personality may be deflected by the Spirit into a new direction. So it proved with the young Francis.

On a pilgrimage to Rome, he was moved with compassion for the beggars outside St Peter's. With that impulsive generosity which was to become second nature to him, he changed clothes with one of the paupers, and began to beg his bread in the streets. This changing clothes with the beggar was for Francis a symbol of his desire to be identified with the neediest of men. He became convinced that to serve the poor and to bring the Gospel to them, he must share their life of poverty himself. As Father Michael Fisher, of the Anglican Society of St Francis, once said of the work of the Brothers in Stepney: 'We believe that if you are ever going to help a man who is in the gutter, you must get down into the gutter with him.' It is the pattern of life followed by Don Mario Borelli when he broke through the barriers of organized religion, to reach the *scugnizzi* (street urchins) of Naples, as Morris West has graphically described in his *Children of the Sun*. It is the spirit of 'Papa Santi', the Methodist minister who filled his orphanage ('Casa Materna') with 350 children from the same Neopolitan slums. One little boy, newly arrived at the great house on the Bay of Naples, and given the first sight of his cheerful bedroom, refused to go to, bed, and screamed to be taken outside. Paper Santi was sent for, and since the child could not be pacified, took him outside—through the gardens and into the village

28

street of Portici. The small boy at once curled up on the pavement and went to sleep, for he had, it transpired, never been in a bed in his life. 'When a child like that comes into my home,' said the old man, 'I do not ask what it feels like to be that child. I *become* that child.' In other words, he so identified with the child, in heart and mind, that he could understand from within something of what life had done to it. Francis was animated by the same impulse, an impulse which stems ultimately from the spirit of Jesus, who though he was rich, for our sakes became poor, that we through his poverty might be made rich. It is the pattern of what Charles Wesley calls God's 'mercy's whole design' in the Incarnation. 'He became what we are,' says Augustine, 'that we might become what He is.'

Francis saw his mission as essentially to the poorest of the poor. In 1208, he heard the call to mission in poverty—'organized destitution' has been described as his ideal—as the Gospel was being read in church. The words were those of Jesus to the Twelve, as he sent them out to preach, and be a sign of, the power of the Kingdom. 'Provide no gold, silver or copper to fill your purse, no pack for the road, no second coat, no shoes, no stick; the worker earns his keep . . .'[8] With the followers of Francis—the friars (frères, brothers)—living in poverty, begging their bread, and preaching the Gospel, there developed a new pattern of mission and religious life. The classic style of religious life in the West had taken its rise from St Benedict and his monks at Monte Cassino. That pattern given on the Mount and embodied in the shrewd, humane Rule of St Benedict, had overspread Europe,

[8] Matthew 10:9, 10

and provided beacons of Christian life and learning in the Dark Ages.

But the High Middle Ages brought a new challenge. Towns and cities were growing all over the continent, crowding the living space within the old city walls, and spilling out into slummy suburbs and townships. They posed a challenge to evangelization which the great Benedictine houses, founded as settled communities and rooted in the tradition of *stabilitas,* could not meet. The flexibility of the Franciscans, travelling light, on the move with the Gospel, was designed to meet it. A glance at the modern Ordnance Survey *Map of Monastic Britain* tells its own tale. The great Cistercian abbeys, following the Benedictine tradition, are located in glorious rural settings—Tintern, Rievaulx, Byland, Fountains. But they were remote from the common life of men, at least the men of the towns. The Franciscan houses, on the other hand, are set in the midst of towns and cities which today, as in the Middle Ages, are among the most significant centres of population: London, Bristol, York, Lincoln, Gloucester, Norwich.

The joy of St Francis, then, sprang from a life of voluntary pauperization, and from serving and suffering with the poorest of the poor. His joy also streamed out of his sense of union with the whole of God's creation. Having nothing, he possessed all things. Because he had nothing of his own, except the robe he stood up in, Francis had an immeasurably heightened joy in the things that were given to all men. He revelled in what was free as air—the earth, the sea and sky, the birds, beasts, flowers and trees. With an inversion of our modern acquisitive lust, he wanted nothing for himself. He was content simply to glory in what God

30

It is as though righteousness and peace, in this biblical understanding, are as utterly bound together as a happily married couple. Without righteousness, or at least the will to righteousness and the attempt to live it out, there can be no peace. It follows, then, that however outwardly quiet a nation, a family, a personal life may be, if it is founded on wrong relationships, its 'peace' is spurious and unreal. The prophets of Israel, and above all Jesus, who speak in the name of the God of righteousness, have to declare unremitting war against such phoney 'peace.' They appear, and must appear, as 'disturbers of the peace.' For them to accept the injustice, the corruption, the perverted relationships—anything for a quiet life—would be a betrayal. They would be crying peace, where there was no peace.

I was once drawn into a pastoral situation involving a strongly Methodist family. It was in some ways more of a clan than a family—large, extended, matriarchal. One of its adult members had been drawn into a morally compromising relationship and the poison was seeping through the life of the family. The old matriarch said to me one day, with an air of quiet finality, 'We don't talk about it. We just live on the surface.' Well, on the surface, no doubt there was calm; but in the hearts of those people there was no peace.

A local paper once reported the case of a man who, in his quiet bungalow on the edge of a country town, had murdered his wife. They had been known to their neighbours as an exceptionally quiet and inoffensive couple. At the trial, however, it came out that they had not spoken to each other for five years. They were certainly a very quiet couple: never a word said in anger; no vulgar brawling or bitter recriminations. The neighbours were never disturbed. All was quiet and at 'peace' thanks to that terrible silence. Until one day the volcanic fires raging underneath, broke surface, and the man took the carving knife and finally vented his hate upon his wife.

If outward quiet can co-exist, in these ways, with deep disturbance, violence, and twisted relationships, just below the surface, then as Euclid would say, the converse is also true. True peace, the *shalōm* which Christ's Spirit brings, can be found in the midst of pain, opposition, strife and conflict. So, in John's interpretation of the mind of Christ, we hear Jesus promising his men: 'Peace is my parting gift to you, my own peace, such as the world cannot give. Set your troubled hearts at rest, and banish your fears.'[3] The context of these words—full of the profound irony of St John—is Jesus' impending passion. The shadow of the Cross is unmistakable. Yet, as he speaks in the midst of danger, betrayal, impending death, Jesus knows and gives true peace.

We turn now to a man, born just over 350 years ago, who is a choice example of a man who knew Christ's peace. He experienced it himself, and transmitted it to others, through a life that was replete with conflict, dangers and suffering.

George Fox (1624–91)

Who was he? Frankly, a nobody in terms of seventeenth-century England. He was one of the common people, one of the great, anonymous toiling mass, the labouring poor. He was humbly born at Fenny Drayton in Leicestershire, the son of a weaver,

[3] John 14:27.

and was himself apprenticed to a shoemaker. His letters reveal the sprawling handwriting and eccentric spelling which betray a minimal amount of schooling. At nineteen, he left his family and friends, and took to the roads as a 'seeker' in search of truth and spiritual enlightenment. In that tumultuous seventeenth-century, such an outward journey, embodying an inner quest, was by no means uncommon, as indeed we might have guessed from Bunyan's spiritual classic. George's 'Pilgrim's Progress' brought him, after three years of intense conflict, to peace and faith through relying on what he came to call the 'Inner Light' of the Risen Christ within his heart. He would have undoubtedly said Amen to the words of Malcolm Stewart's song,

> And today the only stone that rolls away
> to let Him live,
> is inside you.

George Fox was without question a mystic and a prophet of profound spiritual power and originality; a man who was continually seeing visions and dreaming dreams. Yet it would be false to infer from all that an ethereal character, highly strung, and with only a tenuous grip on everyday reality. On the contrary, George was a realist, shrewd, homely, and with striking insight into human nature. Over and over again, he showed that he knew what was in man. There was nothing remote or ineffectual about Fox. To picture him striding the roads of England, we must envisage not a pale curate type, but a big man, young, strong, well set up. He had the physique to take a lot of punishment—and did. 'The man in leather breeches', as he became known, was the bodily equivalent of a strapping young fellow from a modern building site.

Self-taught and Spirit-led, he began to preach his experimental conclusions in religion, with great fire and a zeal that tempered the wind to no man. He was continually imprisoned and persecuted for his attempt to recover original New Testament Christianity. The persecution was a predictable response to the one-man war he carried on against the powers that be, in Church and State. He denounced all ministers of religion who received pay for their work, as hirelings and no true shepherds. He condemned all magistrates for exercising the power of the sword over their fellow man. He recognized no titles or ceremony; refused to swear oaths in court; and would doff his hat to no man, for he held such customs to be a denial of the fundamental equality of all men in God's creation. He denounced existing patterns of religion as formal and dead, and urged men to listen to the Spirit of Christ speaking in their inmost hearts. No intermediary— not Bible, liturgy or minister – must come between the believer and that inward witness of the Holy Spirit.

Seventeenth-century society was shocked to its core by the affront of Quaker criticism and protest. At no point was it more caught on the raw, since Quakerism took its rise in the period of the Civil War and the Commonwealth, than on the question of war and peace. Fox and his followers totally renounced the power of the sword, and would never retaliate against provocation, however violent. Fox took the command that Christians should love their enemies to apply absolutely, not only to personal enemies, but to the enemies of state or society. He became one of the most uncompromising pacifists in Christian history.

To put it mildly, his views gained little popularity among his fellow-countrymen, least of all his witness to the gospel of peace. But he was as good as his word and practised what he preached. Once, when he was being held in custody in Scarborough Castle, a drunken fellow-prisoner challenged Fox to a fight. Fox, recording the incident in his *Journal*, replied, 'I was come to answer him with my hands in my pockets, and . . . there was my hair and my back, and what a shame it was for him to challenge a man whose principle he knew was not to strike; . . . and one of the officers said, "you are a happy man that can bear such things".' At Ulverston, in 1652, he was beaten with stakes and clubs until he fell unconscious. When he came round again, he noted in his *Journal*, 'I lay a little still, and the power of the Lord sprang through me, and the eternal refreshing refreshed me, that I stood up again in the eternal power of God and stretched out my arms amongst them all, and said again with a loud voice, "Strike again, here is my arms and my head and my cheeks", and I was in the love of God to them all that had persecuted me.'

So Fox was no dreamy idealist. His way of life brought him into continual acquaintance with the brutality and viciousness that can corrupt human nature. His very defencelessness and his steadfast following of the way of peace, were an incitement to some of the more bestial characters he met. Yet, though he recognized with prophetic insight the darkness of human sin, he firmly believed that 'The power of the Lord'—his favourite phrase—would overcome evil with good. He was convinced, experientially as well as theologically, that his way of peace was 'the most likely to reach the inward witness and so change the evil mind into the right mind'.[4]

Fox's *Journal* is full of passages which show his shrewdness, plain speaking, and militancy in the Lamb's war. He could deliver a rebuke—like the great Puritans before him and John Wesley after—'plain and home'. He indeed followed Jesus as the humble Lamb of God; but the scripture also speaks of the wrath of the Lamb, and the Gospels show us Jesus cleansing the Temple with the whip of small cords. At one time Fox was imprisoned in Launceston Castle. He was taking his exercise on the Castle Green, when Peter Ceely the local magistrate who had had him arrested, passed by. Ceely took off his hat, with the respectful greeting, 'How do you do, Mr Fox? Your servant, sir,' Fox cut through the smooth civility like a knife: 'Major Ceely, take heed of hypocrisy and a rotten heart, for when came I to be thy master and thee my servant? Do servants use to cast their masters into prison?'

The *Journal* is full of such examples of holy boldness, what the New Testament calls *parrhesia*. This refusal of little people to be overawed by any of the great and mighty of this world, is more than courage. It is more than confidence in the rightness of one's cause. Ultimately it all stems from a serene and unwavering certainty that the Lord God omnipotent reigns; that Jesus is King; and that his Kingdom will have no end. Fox's witness as a man of peace brings home to us the truth of Jesus' word to his disciples, as he sends them out on mission: 'when you come to any town or village, look for some worthy person in it, and

[4] G. F. Nuttall, *The Puritan Spirit*, p. 186. I am also indebted to Dr Nuttall's essay on Fox for the two quotations from his *Journal*.

make your home there until you leave. Wish the house peace as you enter it, so that, if it is worthy, your peace may descend on it; if it is not worthy, your peace can come back to you.'[5] In other words, whatever insults or bad treatment you get, they will not rob you of your inner peace, your sense of quiet integrity. The outward blows will not throw you off balance or disturb your spirit. Fox proved the truth of this promise. He was frequently in mortal danger, but could truthfully say: 'I never feared death nor sufferings in my life.' No one could rob him of his peace.

What does George Fox, the man of peace, say to us today? His pacifism sets a fundamental question mark against all easy sanction of war by the Church. It shows up any kind of crusade or Holy War as the nonsense it must always be in the light of Jesus. At the personal level, he confronts us with an inescapable challenge to love our enemies, turn the other cheek, overcome evil with good. Have we that faith in the Spirit of God as able to speak to the most evil man, through the persistent goodwill, the loving attitude of the followers of the Lamb? Finally, Fox and his followers did not make the way of peace an excuse for condoning evil and injustice. They fought these things passionately—with the sword of the Spirit. Do we? Or do we settle for the spurious peace, which is no peace? If we take our part in Christ's Holy War, we shall find our hearts and minds guarded and garrisoned by his unshakable peace.

SUGGESTED FURTHER READING
George Fox, *Journal*, No. 754 of Everyman's Library (J. M. Dent), edited by Norman Penney (1924)

[5] Matthew 10:11, 12.

Rufus M. Jones, *The Faith and Practice of the Quakers* (1927)

Geoffrey F. Nuttall, *Christian Pacifism in History* (1958)

REFRESHER COURSE EXERCISE

Plan a sermon based on one of the following texts: Ps. 85:10; John 14:27, illustrating, where possible, from the life and work of George Fox.

CHAPTER FOUR

The Fruit of the Spirit is Patience

Dora Greenwell

There is no doubt that ours is an impatient age, when credit cards are readily available to 'Take the waiting out of wanting'. As a girl's name, Patience seems to belong to the age of Gilbert and Sullivan opera, or to an even earlier era. We are obsessed with rapid results, quick returns, instant satisfactions. The miniscule advertisement in some books of stamps used to dazzle us with the invitation: 'Learn to play the piano in ten easy lessons—you will surprise your friends!' No doubt about the latter half of the claim, at all events. Even in the realm of spirituality easy shortcuts are on offer to by-pass the slow, patient disciplines of the inner life. A certain school of Gurus, with the aid of hallucinatory drugs, now proffers the experience of 'Instant Zen', in which no doubt, you will surprise not only your friends, but also yourself.

It is a far cry from the classic Oxford account of the American tourist admiring the immaculate texture of the lawns of an ancient college. 'Say,' asks the tourist of the college gardener, 'how do I get my lawns to look like that?' 'Well, sir, you first sows good seed, and then you cuts 'em and rolls 'em for 600 years—and they just come like that!'

The biblical meaning of patience
The grace of patience, as part of the fruit of the Spirit

in the life of the Christian, is rooted in the patience of God. He bears and forbears with his wayward children. He is long-suffering; knows how to wait; is not easily put off.

> The Lord is compassionate and gracious, *long-suffering* and for ever constant . . .[1]

> Do you think lightly of his wealth of kindness, of tolerance, of *patience*, without recognising that God's kindness is meant to lead you to a change of heart?[2]

The Spirit's gift of patience undergirds each of the three supreme Christian virtues. There is, first, the patience of faith. It consists of a determined trust, a steadfast faith in God and his promises. The classic Old Testament example of it is Abraham, who, 'after patient waiting, attained the promise'.[3] When we speak of the patience of faith, we are not talking about passive resignation, or a stiff-upper-lip stoic acceptance of calmity. It is, rather, a positive determination, despite everything and at whatever cost, to go forward in faith with God. If we can transpose it from its martial context, Churchill's memorable speech of June 1940 has in it something of the temper of Christian patience, though the weapons of our warfare are not carnal:

> We shall not flag or fail, We shall fight in France, we shall fight on the seas and oceans, we shall fight with growing confidence and growing strength in the air, we shall defend our island, whatever the cost may be, we shall

[1] Psalm 103:8
[2] Romans 2:4
[3] Hebrews 6:15

44

fight on the beaches, we shall fight on the landing grounds, we shall fight in the fields and in the streets, we shall fight in the hills; we shall never surrender.

When Douglas Bader lost both legs in a flying accident, his life was at first despaired of. He regained consciousness in hospital to hear one nurse whispering to another, 'Keep your voice down—don't you know there's a boy dying in there?' 'Dying?' he thought to himself, 'we'll see about that.' And see about it he did. When he was offered sticks to help him begin to walk on his artificial legs, he at once threw them away. The doctors remonstrated: 'Don't you realize that no one in your condition has ever begun to walk without sticks?' 'What's that got to do with it?' Bader replied. No doubt there is more than a touch of bravado in that sort of stance. Yet such magnificent spirit has in it more than a little of the patient endurance and determination which belongs to faith.

There is also a patience of hope. Paul refers to it in his letters to Thessalonica, when he extols among the Christians there 'Your labour of love and your patience of hope'.[4] Elsewhere he prays: 'The Lord direct your hearts into the love of God, and into the patient waiting for Jesus Christ.'[5] This patient hope is of a piece with that of the psalmist: 'My soul waits for the Lord, more than watchmen for the morning.'[6] We wait in the patience of hope for Jesus, because he has come, and he will come. He has come—to Bethlehem, Nazareth, Jerusalem, and to our hearts. He will come

[4] 1 Thessalonians 1:3
[5] 2 Thessalonians 3:5
[6] Psalm 130:6

—in whatever joy or sorrow we encounter; at our death, to take us to the Father; and at the end of the world, to sum up all things in himself.

The patience of faith; the patience of hope; and finally there is the patience of love. St Paul distinguishes, as one of the glories of Christian love, the fact that it *'suffers long*, and is kind'.[7] The Greek word for suffers long, *makrothumeo*, implies a patient willingness to endure rejection and ill-usage, without becoming embittered or seeking revenge. The patience of love is especially called for in looking for moral and spiritual growth in children or young people. They may well 'try the patience' of parents or pastors. An irate father once wrote to a Methodist school chaplain, 'Will you, please, *make* my son join your confirmation class?' 'No, indeed I will not,' the chaplain replied, 'I will wait until the boy shows any sign of a desire to join the class, and then I will encourage him.' The patience of love knows that in the end you can compel no one into the Kingdom.

Love learns its patience from Jesus. When he washes his disciples' feet, Peter remonstrates vehemently, before he submits. Jesus assures him, 'You do not understand now what I am doing, but one day you will'.[8] As Willian Temple points out, it is what one could say to any child. So often, as parents, we are impatient, hasty, wanting to force the plant. We expect understanding, awareness, gratitude, beyond any realization of which the child is capable. If we are patient, and sow in faith, in due season we may reap. If we cast our bread on the waters, it may come back to us after many days. If we deal with the child in the

[7] 1 Corinthians 13:4
[8] John 13:7

46

patience of love, 'one day' he will understand—even if it is only when he has become a parent himself.

Dora Greenwell (1821–82)

Dora Greenwell was born at Greenwell Ford, in County Durham, the daughter of the local squire, William Thomas Greenwell, who was a magistrate and Deputy Lieutenant of the County. She had no formal schooling, beyond four years' private instruction from her governess. Apart from this meagre education, she was self-taught. By dint of outstanding natural gifts and voracious reading, she made herself one of the very few women theologians of the nineteenth century. She was heir to a wide European culture, and could read French, German, Italian and Spanish.

An Evangelical Anglican herself, she had a breadth of ecumenical sympathy and understanding which in Victorian England stood out like a good deed in a naughty world. She admired much in the Church of Rome, in the Quakers, and in the people called Methodists. A friend records: 'She loved the Quakers very much, and the Methodists even more, because they are such a strongly social community, and always, as she used to say, "liked going to heaven in parties".'[9] She was a splendid non-Methodist exponent of what John Wesley called 'the Catholic Spirit'.

Yet, with wide intellectual interests and broad religious sympathies, her personal life was cribbed, cabin'd and confined. Her domestic circumstances cramped and constrained her. She was the only girl in the family, with four brothers, so that the weight of

[9] Quoted in W. G. Hanson, *Selections from the prose of Dora Greenwell*, p. 18

domesticity fell squarely on her shoulders. The early nineteenth century knew nothing of higher education for women. Even had family circumstances allowed, there was no prospect of a profession or career. To crown all, her mother, to whom so much of her life was devoted, was a severe trial. Authoritarian, demanding, intolerant, she had no sympathy with Dora's profound spirituality. She lacked all understanding of her daughter's gifts as theologian, poet, prose-writer and spiritual guide. If anyone needed the patience of Job, it was Dora Greenwell.

After the death of her father, to whom she was devoted, Dora moved with her mother from the countryside into Durham City, and looked after the formidable old lady until she died eighteen years later, and the burden rolled off her shoulders. It was a long purgatory. Despite her mother's disapproval, Dora always had prayers in the home. 'A friend has recorded that she heard the terrible old lady exclaim at the hour of devotion: "Prayers, prayers? Whatever do you want with prayers?" Yet she would not absent herself, but would snort and fidget all the time . . .'[10]

Nor were Dora's troubles merely external to herself. Like St Paul she had a 'thorn in the flesh', and her whole life was dogged by ill-health. For her last four years, she moved south-west, to Clifton, near Bristol, but, although the milder climate no doubt helped, these years were overshadowed by great weakness and pain.

In 1860, at the age of thirty-nine, Dora Greenwell published a little book called *The Patience of Hope*. It was written by an authority on the subject if ever there was one. She wrote it not merely in ink, but with her

[10] Henry Bett, *Dora Greenwell*, p. 26

life-blood. She wrote, as John Bunyan preached, 'what she felt, what she smartingly did feel'. Her patience of hope enabled her to overcome the terrible incubus of her family circumstances and ill-health. It empowered her notable achievement in her verse and prose writings. It led her, with quiet persistence, to undertake a range of social and pastoral work which would have daunted many in robust good health. She was a regular visitor to the prisoners in Durham gaol, and 'had many remarkable experiences among the criminals there. She told a friend that she had sat with a murderer's hand clasped in hers, "and felt no fear and no horror".'[11] She worked also among pauper imbeciles, and her article on 'The Education of the Imbecile' proved a landmark in the history of the treatment of the insane. She was a passionate supporter of her friend, Mrs Josephine Butler, in her campaign against the prostitution which was rampant in the cities of Victorian England. Out of all this experience of caring, she could write: 'I have returned to both my jail and penitentiary work. I find there is nothing which is such a sheet anchor to the heart, the soul, and the mind also, as a settled quiet bit of work for Christ'.[12]

The patience with which she coped with her family troubles, and maintained her 'settled quiet bit of work for Christ', was put to another searching test by the bodily sufferings of her closing years. She had then to face what Professor Gordon Rupp has aptly called 'a final honours course in pain'. 'In her last days there were long periods of unconsciousness, from which she emerged to declare emphatically: "He does not fail

[11] Henry Bett, *op. cit.*, p. 25
[12] W. G. Hanson, *Selections from the Prose of Dora Greenwell*, p. 9

me nor forsake me. He does *not*, nay *He never will* fail me." '

She was buried in Arnos Vale cemetery, in Bristol. Her gravestone has a cross incised upon it, together with the Latin inscription, found also on the title-pages of her books: *Et Teneo et Teneor*, I both hold and am held. The motto and the cross are to be taken in the closest relationship, as the books declare. On the standard title page, the cross is grasped by a hand flanked by the Latin motto. She proved those words by the patience of hope with which her life was shot through. Not Stoicism, but the grace of Christ crucified, is the secret of her forbearance, longsuffering, and quiet courage.

We may close with two quotations from her poetry which are alive with her spirit. The first is the last poem in *Carmina Crucis*, a collection of her religious verse:

And art Thou come with us to dwell,
Our Prince, our Guide, our Love, our Lord?
And is Thy name Emmanuel,
God present with His world restored?

The world is glad for Thee! The rude
Wild moor, the city's crowded pen;
Each waste, each peopled solitude,
Becomes a home for happy men.

Thou bringest all again; with Thee
Is light, is space, is breadth and room
For each thing fair, beloved, and free,
To have its hour of life and bloom.

Each heart's deep instinct unconfessed;
Each lowly wish, each daring claim;

All, all that life hath long repressed,
Unfolds, not fearing blight or blame.

Thy reign eternal will not cease;
Thy years are sure, and glad, and slow;
Within Thy mighty world of peace
The humblest flower hath leave to blow.

Then come to heal Thy people's smart,
And with Thee bring Thy captive train;
Come, Saviour of the world and heart,
Come, mighty Victor over pain.[13]

And finally, four lines which have in them so much of the patience of faith, hope and love, which marked her life in Christ Jesus:

Love, love, that once for did agonize,
Shall conquer all things to itself! If late
Or soon this fall, I ask not nor surmise,
And when my God is waiting, I can wait.

SUGGESTED FURTHER READING

Constance L. Maynard, *Dora Greenwell: a Prophet for our own times on the Battleground of our Faith* (1926)

Henry Bett, *Dora Greenwell* (1950)

W. G. Hanson, ed., *Selections from the Prose of Dora Greenwell* (1950)

Dora Greenwell, *Two Friends*, ed. Henry Bett (1952)

REFRESHER COURSE EXERCISE

Plan a sermon based on one of the following texts:
Ps. 103:8; 1 Cor. 13:4a; Heb. 6:15, illustrating, where possible, from the life and work of Dora Greenwell.

---

[13] Also printed in *Methodist Hymn Book*, 259

CHAPTER FIVE

The Fruit of the Spirit is Gentleness

Edward King

The biblical meaning of gentleness

In his hymn 'Gentle Jesus, meek and mild'—which should be judged as a whole, and not by its hackneyed opening couplet—Charles Wesley is transposing into verse part of the Gospel portrait of Jesus. There are two places in the Gospels where the quality of gentleness (in Greek *praytēs*) is used of Jesus. Both are in St Matthew. One is in the great invitation of Matthew 11:29, 'Come to me, all whose work is hard, whose load is heavy; and I will give you relief. Bend your necks to my yoke, and learn from me, for I am *gentle* and humble-hearted.' The second is in Matthew's account of the Entry into Jerusalem: (21:5) 'Here is your King, who comes to you in *gentleness*, riding on an ass.' In the same vein, St Paul writes to the Corinthians, 'I . . . appeal to you by the *gentleness* and magnanimity of Christ . . .'[1]

Yet the quality of gentleness in Jesus is fully compatible with righteous anger and indignation. The gentle Christ is also the one who denounces the money-changers and cleanses the Temple. The 'loving Jesus, gentle Lamb' of Wesley's hymn is also the Lord whose anger blazes out against the miserable hypocrisy and heartlessness of some of the Pharisees. As Edward King was to teach and to exemplify,

[1] 2 Corinthians 10:1

52

'Gentleness is not weakness, but restrained strength'. Samuel Peake, the distinguished biblical scholar and authority on the prophecies of Isaiah, was once assailed, after preaching on the prophet, by an aggressive fundamentalist. 'Professor Peake,' the man hectored him, 'you say there are three Isaiahs, don't you? Well *I* say there's only one!' To which Peake replied quietly and gently, 'Well, that settles it, doesn't it?' He could, of course, from the arsenal of his scholarship, have annihilated his critic. But the soft answer turns away wrath. Gentleness is not weakness, but restrained strength.

Edward King (1829–1910)

For twenty-five years, until his death in 1910, Edward King was Bishop of Lincoln. A man of transparent goodness, he has been described as the most saintly figure the Anglican Church has produced since the Reformation. The great service of thanksgiving held in Lincoln Minster on 24th May 1935, twenty-five years after his death, was one of extraordinary significance in the history of Anglican sanctity. Archbishop Lang preached, at the Choral Eucharist, on 'Edward King, Bishop and Saint'. Collect, Epistle and Gospel were all related to Edward King by name, and from that time his name was added to the Cathedral's Kalendar of Saints. Experts in this field recognize what took place at that service as being as near to a formal canonization of one of her sons as the Church of England has ever come.

King's favourite text was from the Psalter, 'Thy gentleness hath made me great' (Psalm 18:36, in the Authorised Version). It is in many ways the key to his life and goodness, the quality of which so endeared him to the Lincolnshire people, who still treasure his memory. Portraits of him abound—most unusually—in the churches of the diocese, and are treasured in the homes of the people. There is still a living oral tradition of his words and deeds, and a cultus of him as a local saint which puts him in the same category as his predecessor as bishop, the great St Hugh.

Edward King was born in 1829, only fourteen years after Waterloo, as he used to recall, the son of a country rector in Kent. His frail health meant that he was educated privately at home, and became very closely integrated into the life of the family. He was especially close to his crippled sister, and learned Italian so as to be able to share her reading of Dante, of whom he became a lifelong devotee. In 1848, he went up to Oriel College, Oxford, which had raised so many leaders of the High Church movement, and became a firm High Churchman himself. Charles Marriott, one of the outstanding dons at Oriel and a scholarly collaborator of Newman and Pusey, pronounced the enthusiastic verdict: 'King is a royal fellow!'

In his own quiet, unostentatious way, he was devout, and disciplined in his religion. His scrupulous attendance at College Chapel nettled Provost Hawkins, who, in the end-of-term interviews always scraped the barrel to find a word of criticism for each student. 'I observe, Mr King, that you have never missed a single chapel, morning and evening, during the whole term. I must warn you, Mr King, that even too regular attendance at chapel may degenerate into formalism'.[2] No doubt; but King was no formalist. Nor was he a pale recluse or a plaster saint. He was a

[2] G. W. E. Russell, *Edward King* (1912), p. 5

fine horseman, good swimmer, keen fisherman and walker; a man of the open air, well-liked by his fellow students.

After the university, he became curate of the rough, wild parish of Wheatley, near Oxford, where he won the hearts of the country poor, and they found a lasting place in his. Ever afterwards, he was to feel that his real apostolate and pastoral vocation lay among the poor of the countryside. After his few years' curacy, he became first Chaplain, then Principal of Bishop Wilberforce's new theological college, opposite the Bishop's palace, at Cuddesdon. In the 1850s theological colleges were new, controversial, and widely disliked as hot-houses. High Church theological colleges, like Cuddesdon, were stigmatized as Romanizing. But King weathered the storm of criticism, and managed to create a deep fellowship of life in Christ which set an indelible mark on the lives of many of his men. One tough-minded visiting lecturer, who knew Cuddesdon well, spoke of it as, 'A breath of Eden before the door was shut'. King called it, because of its easy relationship between staff and men, 'a Christian higgledy-piggledy'. In Scott Holland's recollection, 'The whole place was alive with him. His look, his voice, his gaiety, his beauty, his charm, his holiness filled it and possessed it . . . He could draw blood out of a stone; and there was not a man of any type of character that did not yield to him.'[3]

In 1873, to his mild amazement, he was taken from Cuddesdon to become an Oxford academic, to wit, the Professor of Pastoral Theology. Some of his lectures have survived, through a student's notebook.

[3] H. Scott Holland, *A Bundle of Memories* (1915), p. 61

From the clipped summary of his living voice we can gauge the quality of his teaching. He urged his ordinands that Christ's 'unchanging love' must be reflected in their ministry, and warned: 'No gentlemanly substitutes for love (e.g. patronage) will do.'[4] Strong, gifted young men, who had never thought of being ordained, were won by King's life and teaching. As his great friend Scott Holland wrote about one such man: 'I saw an "Angel" last night, a Mr—— from some living in Northamptonshire, beautiful, intelligent, thoughtful, charming . . . He knows men, I think; rowed in his boat at Oxford; then got wholly snared by King.'[5]

After twelve creative years in Oxford, Edward King was granted—in a quite unlooked-for way—the chance to work again among the country poor. He was appointed by Mr Gladstone to be Bishop of Lincoln in 1885, and became, as he put it whimsically, 'a big curate in the diocese of Lincoln'. He struck the keynote of his episcopate at the very beginning when he wrote to a friend: 'I am glad it is John Wesley's diocese; I shall try to be a bishop of the poor.' He left the great rambling Palace at Riseholme, and moved into the heart of the city to be near his people. '*Pascite gregem*', feed the flock, was the injunction he carved above the door of his new home. It was this profound sense of pastoral care which broke down barriers wherever he went. He was a strong High Churchman, and so by no means popular with many Anglicans, let alone with the strong Nonconformist population of

[4] *Pastoral Lectures of Bishop Edward King*, ed. Eric Graham (1932), p. 8

[5] *A Forty Years' Friendship: Letters from the Late Henry Scott Holland to Mrs Drew*, ed. S. L. Ollard (1919), p. 37

had poured out on all his sons and daughters, most of whom hardly knew how to value them. While most men lived like paupers in the midst of the fathomless riches of the world—its colour, light, beauty and grandeur—Francis lived the life of a poor man, but as a spiritual millionaire. All created things were to this man matter for joy and for thanksgiving; and, because they pointed beyond themselves to their Maker, matter also for worship and for praise. His great Canticle of the Sun tells it all:

> All creatures of our God and King,
> Lift up your voice and with us sing:
>   Alleluia, Alleluia!
> Thou burning sun with golden beam,
> Thou silver moon with softer gleam:
>   O praise Him, O praise Him,
>   Alleluia, Alleluia, Alleluia![9]

Yet it would be a mistake to assume that St Francis' life was simply a sunny idyll, as he revelled in the joy of the natural world. For him, Creation and Redemption were intimately bound together in the loving purposes of God. Dom David Knowles focuses the essential life and character of Francis as 'a revelation of the imitation of Christ crucified, in love and suffering'. For a certainty, Francis knew all about 'the joy that followest me through pain', as the stigmata he bore profoundly betokened.

Brother Leo, in a famous conversation, once asked of Francis: 'Father, I pray thee teach me wherein is perfect joy.' Francis replied: 'If when we shall arrive at St Mary of the Angels, all drenched with rain and trembling with cold, all covered with mud and

[9] *Methodist Hymn Book,* 28, v. 1

exhausted from hunger—and are beaten and driven away repeatedly—. . . if we bear all these injuries with patience and joy, thinking of the sufferings of our Blessed Lord, which we would share out of love for Him, write, O Brother Leo, that here, finally, is perfect joy.'[10]

It stands to sense that poverty alone does not produce profound spirituality or glad thanksgiving. It may far more readily create in a man envy, malice and all uncharitableness. For Francis, however, his poverty and suffering were all experienced 'in Christ', and so served to bind him to his Lord and to the poor with whom the Lord is one. To lose his life—for Christ and the poor—was to find it again, immeasurably enriched, full, pressed down and running over. It was precisely as a fool for Christ's sake, *Le jongleur de Dieu*—God's jester—that Francis found his joy. The *poverello*, as he called himself—God's little poor man—is Chaplinesque in his archetypal capacity for being knocked down and trampled on and still coming up for more. But unlike Charlie, that superb, secular *poverello,* Francis comes up smiling and singing, radiating joy.

G. K. Chesterton's essay on Francis gets nearer to the core of his spirit than even Norman MacCaig's poem. The paradox of joy in and through suffering, as far as Francis is concerned, could hardly be better expressed than in Chesterton's picture of the death of the saint.

St Francis devoured fasting as a man devours food. He plunged after poverty as men have dug madly for gold

[10] *The Little Flowers of St Francis,* ed. Hugh Martin, SCM Press (1956), pp. 65, 66

... It is certain that he held on this heroic or unnatural course from the moment when he went forth in his hair-shirt into the winter woods to the moment when he desired even in his death agony to lie bare upon the bare ground, to prove that he had and that he was nothing. And we can say, with almost as deep a certainty, that the stars which passed above that gaunt and wasted corpse stark upon the rocky floor had for once, in all their shining cycles round the world of labouring humanity, looked down upon a happy man.[11]

SUGGESTED FURTHER READING

G. K. Chesterton, *St Francis of Assisi* (1923)

John R. H. Moorman, *St Francis of Assisi* (New Edition 1976)

John R. H. Moorman, *Richest of Poor Men: The spirituality of St Francis of Assisi* (1977)

REFRESHER COURSE EXERCISE

Plan a sermon based on one of the following texts: Hab. 3:17–18; 1 Pet. 4:12–13, illustrating, where possible, from the life and work of St Francis of Assisi.

[11] G. K. Chesterton, *St Francis of Assisi,* pp. 96–7

CHAPTER THREE

The Fruit of the Spirit is Peace

George Fox

The biblical meaning of peace
Given a word-association test, we may well find
that the word 'peace' conjures up for us all that makes
for a quiet life. We picture a sheltered spot, a cottage
in the country, and a life free from noise, distraction,
worry and overwork. But the biblical words for
peace (Hebrew, *shalōm*: Greek, eirēnē), have
an infinitely deeper and subtler meaning than
that.

'There is no peace . . . for the wicked'[1] says Isaiah,
usually quoted by the harassed housewife, overwhelmed by the cares of home, work and family. Is
there really no peace for the wicked in the popular
sense? Clearly there is. The wicked man's business
may flourish like the green bay tree. He may thrive on
tax-evasion, and take frequent trips to his villa in the
South of France. But peace? That he cannot know, if
by peace we mean *shalōm*. He cannot know it,
because it is bound up with goodness and straight
dealing and right relationships. As the psalmist
exclaims:

Mercy and truth are met together;
Righteousness and peace have kissed each other.[2]

[1] Isaiah 48:22
[2] Psalm 85:10

Return to
Blood Creek

Frank Callan

A Black Horse Western

ROBERT HALE

© Frank Callan 2018
First published in Great Britain 2018

ISBN 978-0-7198-2717-4

The Crowood Press
The Stable Block
Crowood Lane
Ramsbury
Marlborough
Wiltshire SN8 2HR

www.bhwesterns.com

Robert Hale is an imprint
of The Crowood Press

The right of Frank Callan to be identified as
author of this work has been asserted by him
in accordance with the Copyright, Designs and
Patents Act 1988

All rights reserved. No part of this publication may be
reproduced or transmitted in any form or by any means,
electronic or mechanical, including photocopying, recording,
or any information storage and retrieval system, without
permission in writing from the publishers.

St Helens Libraries	
3 8055 25003 2794	
Askews & Holts	31-May-2018
AF	£14.50

ONE

It was a summer's day with enough heat to trouble a lizard, and Cal Roney screwed up his face to squint into the distance. He was hoping to see the first buildings in Long Corral, because he had taken enough pain from Wyoming already that day since bedding down in the open the previous night and then starting out early. The appaloosa was tired out as well, and it was high time there was some chow in front of them both, with a long, cold drink in the deal.

He was tall, carrying a little extra round the midriff since the cow-herding days stopped, but he was fit and strong enough. He still kept the same bandanna he had worn when working the Shawnee Trail, along with the plainsman and his favourite weapon, the Remington Army .44. He was swarthy, well tanned after the years on the drives; he was crowding fifty but still fired with a passion for the range and for doing something useful. There had been too much time wasted when he was a young-ster, always in scrapes and always having to use his fists. He thought about his appearance now he was heading that way. Luckily his face was full of hair, and he could pull the hat down low – and he would need to do that in the next few hours.

Since he left Laramie, his memory kept going back to the meeting with the agent, Don Lerade. It had been a slightly nervous affair, as rumour was circulating that the Pinkertons were cutting back on work in the frontier. But he had been called to the office and he stood there, hat in hand, on best behaviour. Lerade had looked over the file the Agency kept on all the men working with them. He was a swarthy, tanned man who looked as though he had been born in the plains and had lived among the native tribes. Or maybe, Cal had thought, he had some Mexican in him. He looked every inch the general, with the kind of stature and straight back that went with command. He perused the file and then looked up, 'So, Roney, you know this territory pretty well?'

He had confirmed that, and listened while Lerade described the assignment. 'Young man, no hesitation in using a gun . . . bring him in.'

Lerade kept his thoughts to himself, but in truth he was doubtful. This was Roney's second assignment, and the first had not worked out too well, though he was a fast learner. The Pinkertons were very particular about their recruits, and they did like army men, but they had to be the right kind of army men. They knew that often the best, toughest soldiers are not necessarily the most suitable detectives. A man handy with his fists was fine, and accuracy firing a gun was also fine, but the intelligence of a hunter, combined with the sixth sense of a scout were ideal.

Cal had never really liked Lerade. He was too fussy and proud. But a commander was a commander and you did the job. In the little preparatory session before the trip, Lerade had gone through the details better than any sergeant-major. 'You are a Pinkerton detective, and that means anonymity here. You are no longer Calhoun Roney . . . no, you are William Boldwood, a businessman on his way west. If ever you have to explain yourself, talk about mining and excavations. Let's say you invented a new sluice for sifting the rock and dirt of its gold or silver . . . you see the point? I'm saying that you need to lie convincingly. This is a primary Pinkerton skill, Cal. You understand?'

He had understood. In fact, it was like acting a part – amateur dramatics – like his ma had done a few times, way back when he was small enough to ride a big hound. Yes, he would need to lie.

He had started, alone, wondering why it had been so much of a trial, facing Lerade. After all, he had worked for the Agency for a little while. Fact was, Cal never trusted the men who sat behind desks. He was a man who liked to be riding, chasing the next weather. But this time he was, in part, chasing his own past.

He trudged on, thinking that he must be close to the town now, and the horizon kept deluding him. But that was what a long ride was all about: shutting off the desire to think and to plan. The secret was to endure the trials of a long ride by settling the mind into its own little dream. Reality could wait. It was a turning-point for him, this assignment at Blood Creek. He had come to see that crossroads are not only on the maps: they tend to crop up as you ride through life, too. He was coming to one now, he thought, as the great immensity of the frontier stretched ahead. The trail up or across the frontier was like nothing else, like no other journey; it could offer joy and delight in equal measure with pain and suffering. Yet it always had the scent of the unknown adventure. He had learned to smell that scent, as sharp as the stink of some hunted creature in the open, scared for its life.

Then there it was: Long Corral. He had tried his hardest when he met the Pinkerton boss in Laramie to avoid this job, but there was nobody else, and the target had been sighted, as they put it, settled in Blood Creek with a woman and a fat man with a crocked leg from the war. Result being that, as he told himself again now he was close, he would have to ride through the town, and in fact he would have to rest there before going on. There was nowhere else, and both he and the horse would drop dead unless they took some easy time pretty soon.

Working in Cheyenne and around Laramie had been fine for years: far enough away from a number of places where he wasn't welcome, and that reputation had all been down to his antics before the Pinkertons signed him up. Trouble stuck to him like a burr: his pa had said that, and it had been the only thing the old man ever got right. There was no explanation, but sheer bad luck: Cal Roney attracted trouble like a carcass brought the vultures.

Trouble, he thought, is something that comes in disguise as a rule. It always came to Cal Roney in the form of its opposite – it could be a cultured gentleman in a smart suit, who turned out to be a hired killer; or it could come as a perfumed lady, running a gambling saloon on the river, and she was just as deadly as the hired killer.

Trouble had crossed his path wherever he went: he had gone to war to fight the South, and then he had strayed to Texas and joined the drives north, where trouble wore the appearance of the Comanches. Then he had run into trouble again in every saloon and beer shop between the Pecos and the Platte. No paperwork told this story: it was written in the scars on his hard, weather-beaten body.

But it was a good ten years since he had been in that tight corner in this God-forsaken stretch of the territory. Maybe most of the men who would remember him were dead and gone and feeding the weeds. It was the kind of tight corner that a man dreaded. The kind that takes away an innocent person, a passer-by; it was the kind of tight corner that blackened a man's reputation, and, worst of all, it told a story about him that was a deep, painful lie. And a lie, spread around the settlements strung along borders and fingers of the trails, had a habit of turning into a truth and a hard fact in folks' minds.

Maybe those minds had forgotten, though, as time had eaten away at memories. Still, a twinge of apprehension ran through him as the horse slowed and they trotted towards the place he needed – the Heath Hotel, as it used to be called.

As Cal was closing in on town, a man was scrabbling out of a hole, tugging at another man's arm, a man down in the chasm beneath Long Corral jail. 'Come on Jakey, shift it will ya? The horses are over the way there and we need to be out of this stinking dive of a town!'

'I ain't as slippery and quick as you, big brother . . . I got my bad leg, you recall?'

'Hell with the bad leg . . . we get snapped up here, we get our necks stretched. You savvy? Now shift!'

10

The timing was perfect. The deputy on watch always went for his food at a regular time, and there was a gap of ten minutes for the brothers to get out of there.

The men breaking out had been well prepared for the escape, as men from their kin had worked on the planks outside at dead of night, and from inside, a swift and determined series of blows soon loosened the wood and made a square foot of fresh air. Then outside, a few feet of ditch had been made. Through most of the county, jails had been made real cheap, as every citizen knew, and the way out was usually by brute force against wood. The Kenny clan were skilled at this kind of business.

The younger man finally made it, after digging out the last roots and chunks of cement, and then sprinted for the road. But their escape had been noticed now, and a group of men from the saloon had been rousted by the Deputy Sheriff, Ben Stile, who now stood in the middle of the dirt road and yelled out 'Right, Jake Kenny, stop right there and raise your hands.' He had not seen big brother Eddie, who now stopped running and turned to face the lawman. He screamed, 'That's the last time you give the Kenny boys an order!' He drew his pistol and prodded his right arm forward. But as his finger squeezed the trigger, the deputy was hit by the flying body of Cal, who had ridden up behind and thrown himself at the man, to push him wide of

11

the bullet's trajectory. But as Cal was reaching out and kicking himself into the air, the bullet rapped into his shoulder and he felt a stab of agonizing pain before he hit the dust and then rolled towards the front of a sidewalk, his head slamming into the hard planks.

The Kenny brothers met no further obstacles. They ran to the livery where their youngest brother Jim was waiting with the horses. The crowd of citizens parted for them and women shrieked with fear. Someone shouted 'Stop them!' but there was no soul bold enough in Long Corral to take on all three Kenny boys.

Folk rushed to help their deputy to his feet. He was unharmed apart from a bruise or two, but his saviour was out cold.

'He saved your life, Ben ... knocked flat out when he hit that post!' This was Macky Heath, the man whose hotel Cal had been making for. 'Someone fetch the doc!'

Cal was soon lying on a couch in a back room of the Heath Hotel, and Doc Heath was there, making ready to take the slug out of the arm. He bandaged Cal's head and covered a wound on one cheek with a thick pad to cushion the wound. 'He's a brave man ... anybody know him?' said Emilia Stile, the deputy's sister, who was acting as nurse for the doc. Cal was now coming round and trying to speak. He was sweating and trying to lift his arms to push

12

himself up. The doc told two men to hold him down.

'Now son, I'm gonna take this slug out. . . there'll be some hurtin' but you should live to see another day. Right?'

'Where's my horse . . . where's Bella . . . where's my mare?'

'We got your hoss in good hands, now hold tight and think of somethin' far away,' said the doc. 'Somebody might bring whiskey!' he added, with more force. Emilia whispered in Cal's ear that he would be OK, but she was mopping up blood as she spoke. In went the pliers and there was a tight-lipped groan from Cal, who then passed out as the bullet was lifted free from its entanglement in a knot of muscle.

'Missed the artery by the breadth of a pin!' Doc Heath said, leaving him in Emilia's good hands. Deputy Stile had been overseeing the proceedings, and now, with Cal out cold, he asked if anybody knew the man. There was no reply. Later Cal would realize how glad he was that his face was mostly covered with the bandages and with long, dirt-caked hair. Stile, who might have remembered him, saw too little face to recognize.

'Well, he saved my skin, and I'd like to know who the hell he is, and where he came from. I've never been one for praying and for spending time in that church up the road, but maybe I believe in

guardian angels now. That slug was meant for me.'
Ben Stile was a square, solid man of forty. He had
seen some of the worst of the war and had come out
of it with a burning desire to see some open space
and have plenty of room around him for raising a
family. Sheriff Capp was away in Cheyenne and the
town was in his hands, but he had the Kenny brothers to cope with, and they had very nearly rubbed
him out. Stile hung around as the other townsfolk
finally moved away, and he sat by Emilia and the
patient, hoping the man would come round. She
put a fresh bandage on his face, as blood had soiled
the first.

'He's got the look of a veteran . . . maybe a good
few years on me, I reckon. See that old wound
there, girl? We found a pocket book on him . . .
name's William Boldwood.'

Emilia looked over her patient's bare chest and
settled her gaze on Cal's neck. 'He's been cut by
something . . . maybe a sword. Reckon he's a
soldier?' Ben Stile nodded. They studied a man who
had seen some violence, and his body had plenty
more wounds under his pants and boots. 'I don't
care who he is . . . I owe him my life and he's gonna
get due recompense, Emilia my dear. Under the
bandages and wounds, and all that damned hair, I
can't see the man rightly at all!' He went back to his
office, telling his sister to let him know as soon as
the man came round and could speak.

That happened about an hour later. He tried to move, but then groaned in pain. Emilia held his hand and padded his face with cool water. The fear now was that he would become feverish. He wasn't able to utter anything that made any sense, and that continued for hours. By dusk he slept a little, and Emilia made herself some coffee. The doc came to check on their patient, and with an anxiety that was obvious he felt the pulse and then listened to Cal's breathing. The doc frowned. 'Emilia . . . you staying with him? Good, then call for me if you're worried at all.'

Darkness fell. The young woman sat by her patient, watching his every movement and listening to his breathing, noting any change in the noises he was making. She had nursed plenty of folk before that day, being twenty-nine and devoted to her brother and his family, while having none of her own. She was, as everyone in Long Corral tended to say, surely a half-sister to Ben Stile, or maybe a throw-back, as he was the epitome of a Norwegian, a Viking: fair-haired and angular, and folk said he could have passed for an old sea-dog.

Emilia was different in every way. She was what folk thought of when they figured a person was Italian, and she was indeed a dark beauty, a woman who had refused the hands of three local men, preferring time with books and learning to any version of courting and wooing. Truth is, some called her

15

Miss Doc as she studied the anatomy books and tended to cut up dead critters to learn about their bones and such.

Emilia passed the time with a mix of prayer and the administration of little comforts, as the night wore on. She dropped off to sleep at one time, and when she woke, she poured more coffee. Then, as dawn was no more than a pinhole of light flickering on the curtains, her patient woke and said, 'Howdy Miss. . .where am I?'

'You're in good hands.'

'My chest hurts like hell, and my shoulder has spasms shootin' through it.'

'You took a bullet . . . saving my brother's life. I'm Emilia Stile . . . pleased to meet you, William!' She held out a hand and smiled at him.

Without taking a second to use his brain and agree with the word William, he said, 'No. . . . No . . . I'm Cal Roney . . . pleased to meet *you*!'

The words put a shiver of apprehension into her. She pulled away and her body stiffened. Cal read her movements and when she repeated his name, he had an inkling that something was badly wrong.

'You're Cal Roney? That what you said?'

'Yes . . . that's my name.'

'You're not William Boldwood?'

As she spoke the words, Cal knew exactly what his mistake had been.

She tried to hide her shock then. But Cal

16

guessed. The beard and the hair might have hidden the secret if he had kept his mouth shut, but now he had blurted out his real name without thinking.

'Cal Roney . . . I've heard that name, and not in a good way, mister! My brother told me about Cal Roney . . . he was responsible for a woman's death. Are *you* that Cal Roney?'

Cal felt the shock of the words he was hearing, and all his shame, despair and confusion rushed back into him, deep down where his bad feelings had been gnawing at him for more than ten years. Something inside him made him grab at the woman's wrist and say, desperately, 'Miss, miss, please don't tell anyone. I swear on the holy book, I did not cause that woman's death. I swear it!'

She looked at his hand and then into his eyes. He released his hold. 'I'm so sorry miss, I didn't mean no harm. You have to believe me . . . what happened wasn't like the papers said . . . your brother got it all wrong.'

Emilia weighed the fact that she had seen this man save the life of her brother with the dark reputation that smeared the name he had spoken from inside the wrath of his fever. He looked so weak, so dependent on her, that she nodded and agreed. 'Fine. I'll say nothing, Cal Roney. But you have to see that I've been trusting in my brother Ben's words for a very long time.'

He raved some more and then slept, though fit-fully. As he lay still for a while, the woman looked closely at the stranger and her mind was tormented with the feelings her promise had made in her. He *looked* good, and that was nonsense, as she knew. But Emilia Stile believed in instinct, and she had faith in her convictions. He *did* look good. Here was a man who had risked his neck for a stranger, and had acted with a heroism rare as a sober tramp. She owed him the benefit of the doubt, and when Doc Heath arrived as the morning light told her that it was time to eat or wash or both, he asked about the patient.

As she answered, her words were confirming the lie she had agreed upon. 'Mr Boldwood has been through the worst of the fever. I've been real worried, Doc.'

Doc Heath had a close look at Cal and then managed a slight smile. 'There are reasons to be optimistic, Emilia. You've done a good job, as I knew you would. Now go and get some rest yourself. Macky's fixing you some grub.' He could see that she was in urgent need of sleep, and he insisted that she go.

As Emilia paused at the door, the stranger's eyes opened again and he sat up as if waking from a bad dream. Doc Heath held him and told him to rest some more. But before Emilia walked out, Cal shouted out, 'Get the infantry out of there now . . .

18

get 'em out. They'll be dead meat!'

He fell down again and Doc Heath said, 'Easy, mister, easy. You're in good hands.'

He might or might not be a good man, Emilia thought, but he's seen some things that scar a man's soul. For the time being at least, his secret was safe with her. Cal buried his head in the pillow, still forcing out some words and some nonsense in his delirium. He hadn't planned it, but this was the most effective way of hiding his real appearance. Nobody took much interest in a man raving and raging. He had Emilia on his side, too, and so far, he had stayed anonymous.

TWO

Lerade in Laramie was still plagued by doubts about the Blood Creek job. Could Roney handle that by himself? Maybe he should have sent an experienced man with him? He was having these doubts as he sat in his office, sitting back and forwards in his massive armchair, and looking through the maps and papers collected on the robbery concerning the man now at Blood Creek. The robber had been young, fearless, quite prepared to put a gun barrel in a bank teller's face. Could Roney deal with this?

Maybe he had miscalculated, he thought, and he might even be putting Agent Roney's life at risk. He pondered on the main points of his information on the area, and he recalled that the power around there was in the hands of the Kenny ranch. They had been garnering steers from here, there and everywhere, building up a very large herd. Reports noted that they were employing more and more hands as well, mopping up plenty of the rovers and rustlers created by the end of the war.

Lerade got to his feet and paced around the room. He almost laughed at himself, fretting so much about one fairly routine mission – at least on paper. But it was the apparently manageable ones that turned out to be big trouble, in his experience. After half an hour of this deliberating and worrying, he decided to call in Matt Calero, his most perceptive and battle-hardened agent.

Calero was there by the time Lerade had brewed up some strong coffee, and when his man sat down, his leathery face lined and mobile with every word spoken, Lerade had an immediate sense of comfort and reassurance. Calero knew Texas and New Mexico best as he had served around the Pecos when younger, and had seemed to know about Roney when the job at Blood Creek was first mentioned. He was short but wiry, and knew horses better than any man in Pinkerton's northern operations. His hair was like a porcupine, brushed back and oiled; his clothes were always immaculate when he was in town and not working, and his only flaw was a fondness for the tables and indulging in too much faro with too little cash and too much bravado.

'So I'm just a little concerned about Roney. Matt, please confirm: can he do this job?'

'I wouldn't have given you my recommendation

if I thought he couldn't. He's tougher than *vaquero* leather, though not so polished! What's eatin' you, Lerade?'

'Ah, it's probably nothing . . . it's only that he's new . . . and there's that Blood Creek story . . . bad luck and such.'

'You don't believe all that surely? Tales like that are spread around when some folk don't want settlers and drifters coming their way . . . you *do* know that, boss?'

'Sure. Drink some coffee and tell me I'm a fool.'

He did just that. But before he left, as he was walking to the door, Lerade said, 'Matt, to be sure, keep in touch with someone at Long Corral, hey? The hotel maybe. There's the Heath brothers there. They know me.'

Calero cracked his face with a smile of amusement and took his orders with an assurance that there was nothing to fret about. Cal Roney was a sound man, dependable. He was more than dependable, he knew, but said nothing. In fact, he owed his life to Cal Roney.

In the log house out at Blood Creek, Sedge Gulley was putting the finishing touches to breakfast. His movements could be heard beyond the kitchen, as his wooden leg rumbled and dragged along the planks, and he sang. In fact he couldn't help singing. The habit had grown in his days as cook for the drives down on the Western Trail. He was a fine advert for rich, wholesome food, as he was as broad as he was high, over sixty years carried in his frame, and his head was bald as a coot.

He had relished playing cook, stand-in grandpa and general servant to the young couple he had met on the road the other side of Cheyenne. They had been part of a line of wagons following the Platte all the way from the Mississippi, but by the time they reached Cheyenne, it was breaking up and most had dug in somewhere. They had been as lost as Sedge himself, and they naturally fell in as friends. He had taken enough of the life on the drives, but even settled there at Blood Creek, his old habits died hard. What he did when organizing his buckboard he did now in the lean-to: everything was in its place, and he could knead the bread on a drop-down board, brew up coffee strong as mud, and bake biscuits and puddings to his heart's content. Cy had told him he would have made a good mother, and Sedge said what he had said a thousand times on the trails: 'A cook and his cowhands are a mother hen and her chicks . . . but the cook does all the cluckin', you follow?'

This morning he looked around at the beauty of the place: the sweep of water and the hills beyond, and the little island in the centre of the water, a place known to locals as Cary Island after the old hunter who lived in there, a recluse. It was an assembly of huge rocks, with dense vegetation around and in between: a perfect natural fortress, and old Cary was reputed to have fallen out of love with all mankind, shut himself in there, and turned miserable as a Montana winter.

'Get in here! Grub up . . . get in here!' He yelled in the doorway, looking out to the shack where Cy and Lizzy were mending the old door. Lizzy, no more than a gangly girl, was holding the edge of the door while Cy hammered in some nails. They had settled in the place six months back, newly wed, after looking for somewhere away from any sort of crowd and from the law. The young wife was fair-haired, rake-thin and bronzed. She was short, but strong and tough. There had been no illusions about what she was getting into. Cy Felder had been on the wrong side of the law since she first met him, when they were both no higher than a yearling's mane.

Cy lifted the door away and propped it against the shack wall. 'Yeah . . . come on, Lizzy. Let's eat.' He put his arm around her, and she felt that strength in him that had always drawn her to his side. He was strong as a bull and over six feet. He had earned his living by anything from bare-fist fighting to stage robbing, and this was catching up with him: before they even arrived at Blood Creek, he had known that the law was on his trail. He now deeply regretted what he had done, and he had crossed the line into crime in extreme need. The money kept those around him from starvation. But the law would only see the case as a bold and dangerous robbery.

They sat around the old table in the shack, close to the lean-to where Sedge kept his food supplies and cooking materials. Lizzy did what she always did when they sat down: she complimented Sedge on the dinner. 'It's real tasty, Sedge, as usual. I reckon them cow punchers never had empty bellies when you worked the trails.'

'Well, you keep a good supply of sourdough, bacon fat and coffee, and you got the basis of fine eatin' – though of course, a man's gotta bake bread every day, keep a jug of syrup handy and be a little enterprisin' with the basic stuff.'

Lizzy was talkative, but they could both see that Cy was brooding on something. Sedge asked what was eating him.

'Truth is, Sedge, it's been a few months now since we settled in here, and the fact is, the Pinkertons don't give up. I'm expectin' them any day now.'

Sedge was keen to keep things peaceful. 'Look, son, you know I've had some good luck along the way in my travels . . . except for this damned leg at that fool-headed scrap at Palmito. I mean dammit, the war was all signed off and done with, and that Teddy Barrett had to get some battle in him afore we was all bound for home. . . .'

'Yes. You said once that you nearly drowned, Sedge?' Lizzy asked.

'Sure. A number of us drowned in the Rio Grande . . . I saw two men go under. That was four years back. Now here we are, close to a new decade, and that day's as fresh as new-picked fruit . . . I made it to the bank and then got the bullet that put a stop to my runnin' days. I been walkin' ever since. But what I'm saying, Cy, is that even the Pinks get bored. Just take it easy. We're on the side of a lonesome creek, a day's ride from Laramie, and there's not a soul knows about us. If we go on shootin' most of the meat for the table, we're fine.'

'Yes, but we still need provisions from Long Corral, Sedge,' put in Lizzy. 'Folk know us there. If strangers come and ask questions . . . well, we'll have the wrong kind of visitors here. Cy's right. We're an easy target. Maybe we should move on soon. You could be right about the time. I mean when 1870 comes along, we could all have a fresh start.'

'Aw, to hell with movin' on. Look, I'm too long in the tooth to go shiftin' on again. I been a soldier, a cowboy, a cook, and now I'm everybody's grandpa. Of course, you two are all I got. You're my whole family! I just need some roots dug in here. Now eat that soup and wind down some . . .'

'Another month, Sedge. If that's still quiet, I'll

accept that the law's forgotten me.' Cy said. 'Course, I robbed a bank. The idle rich don't forget that. Then there's the Pinkerton pride. They never give up. The whole frontier knows that!'

'You didn't harm nobody, Cy, and God knows you did it to keep us in food and pay some rent. You were on the edge that time. You're not a bad man, Cy,' Lizzy said.

'No, but I walked away with five hundred bucks and I put the fear of God in a few old men in fancy suits.'

'Well, who's liable to look twice at an old-timer like me, ugly as a mud fence and with a brain addled by too much paintin' my tonsils? Just keep your beautiful wife out of sight and we'll be fine. She's the honey that might bring in the drifters.'

'Drifters we can handle, Sedge. But it's the lawmen that bother me. Yes, we got water and we got wood here. Over on the plains some folk might kill for these, but here, well, for me, it might be called Blood Creek, but it's only a spit away from Paradise.' Cy gave Lizzy a hug, and she kissed his cheek. 'Try not to worry, darlin' . . . it'll be all right.'

They ate and talked, and then Sedge sang a few songs from his days on the drives. He told a few tales he had told a dozen times before, but they didn't mind and they still listened like children by the fire on a winter's evening. When the young folk went off to bed, he went outside to stare at the moon and

27

whisper a prayer to whatever guardian angel had seen him through the War and through the cattle drives. Sedge was too old a warrior to believe in the power of blind faith. He knew that Cy was right: that any night now, there would be someone out there in the cottonwood trees and the scrub who wanted Cy Felder in a jailhouse.

In the office that joined Octavius Gibbs's home on the edge of Long Corral, the stars in that late night had another pair of eyes looking up and contemplating the future. This was Gibbs himself, newspaperman, owner and manager of the *Long Corral Informer* and long-time aspirant to a certain level of celebrity in the literary world.

Gibbs was known as 'Sonny' because once, way back before life kicked him down, he was a man with a hearty disposition and a light-hearted tendency to tell entertaining tales of the frontier from the days when the real hard cases took on the elements and the natives and never felt a tremble of fear. He was thin, hollow-cheeked and long-legged, stretching to over six feet; he was self-regarding, likely to lecture folk or even preach, and a touch lyrical, as when younger he was branded with poetry, men said, deep in him as any steer with a Double T imprint.

When he had first come west, Gibbs had been brimming with ideas about taking some kind of fine living out there: making places where folk could talk about reading and writing, plays and concerts. He still fooled himself that he was promoting such things, but in truth he was having to fill the paper with paragraphs on diseases of cattle, projects about new stage-lines, mining up the territory and then even reports on ladies' meetings, church suppers and the box parties of the young unmarried maidens of Long Corral. He had filled in the cultural and literary space with pieces written by him in various pen-names, and he enjoyed being 'Lawrence Delany, poet' or 'Constantine Doughty, tragic actor.'

It was the Double T that kept a dark cloud over Sonny Gibbs. That was the outfit run by the Kenny brothers, who since their pa died a year back, had acted like they owned every inch of land between Laramie and the Platte to the west of town. That domain included Long Corral, but it was not theirs yet, and in their way stood Sonny and the Heath brothers, backed by Stile. Gibbs prayed every night that the lawman would stay on the side of the town, and that the Heaths would stay and resist. Weaker men would have caved in and run out north, high-tailing it to Casper maybe.

On this night, though, his thoughts were of his dead wife, Ellen, gone now ten years, and the anniversary of that fateful date was coming up soon. Again, for the thousandth time, the events of that

29

day ran through his mind as he looked up to the heavens and tried to think of stars, not the melancholy of loss down here on this planet where men have to struggle and time eats away everything.

He saw the rider coming into town and shouting for Cal Roney to come out and face him. It had been a day so hot that hands could be browned just pressing on boards or leather, and the stranger riding into town was known to all the townsfolk. He was the hellcat father of the Kenny boys, Nathan Kenny, a man familiar with the Devil and all his works, and that night he shot his rifle into the jail door and yelled again for Roney, and then for Stile, to come out and fight. It had been Roney who walked out. At that time he fancied himself as a gunslinger, and men were coming to take him on after he dealt with the Segram twins in Laramie. He had rubbed out the best guns between Cheyenne and the Medicine Bow range. Kenny wanted him.

He had walked out into the dusk, the tall and rugged figure of Cal Roney, and his hands hovered over his two pistols, ready to respond if Kenny pressed him too far. That was exactly what had happened. Kenny lifted his carbine around, and Roney pulled out both guns. Bullets could have riddled Kenny's chest and put him down dead, but Roney had purposely shot wide and low, accepting the pleasure of terrifying his opponent rather than killing him. But behind him, Ellen Gibbs was walking, carrying a basket of cakes for her wives' meeting, where they were sewing a quilt. She never made another stitch. She died so fast, by the time Sonny Gibbs was across the road and kneeling over her, she was gone.

He had lowered his head to her chest and his sobs came through him in waves of sorrow before he screamed out her name to the sky. Then he turned to Roney, who was standing behind him with Ben Stile and a gathering crowd, and as Doc Heath crouched and listened for any sign of breath, Roney had groped for words to express his feelings, but all Gibbs could do was rush at him and crack him on the jaw. Roney had taken a rain of punches and not retaliated.

Then came the inquest and the verdict of accidental death. His Ellen had lain there, on a table, to be identified, and Roney, standing at the back, had left town, and had not been seen since. Even Nathan Kenny, rat that he was, had been spared that day – but his wife had died.

Gibbs was sensing tears on his cheeks, as he saw that death again, running through his mind, and he was interrupted by his neighbour, Mary Collin, who had brought him some dinner earlier. It was still there, on the sideboard.

'Why, Mr Octavius. . . you've not touched the pie. It's my special mix. You need to eat!'

Gibbs turned and looked at Mary, who carried

seventy years light as a bag of feathers, standing there with her fraying old apron and her hair in a high bun, seeing just how much she tried to care for him. A twinge of guilt ran through him, and on his face Mary saw the story of what had been shaking his thin frame like a storm.

'Mr Octavius . . . you don't have to explain. I know what date it is, and I know that in two days it's going to be ten years since we lost her . . .'

'Thank you, Mary. Leave the food . . . I'll eat it cold.'

'You should sleep now. You've been up and busy since six this mornin' – but I'm not going to preach at you, 'cause I know you got your own frazzled brain runnin' you loco.'

Before she left to leave him to his thoughts, he almost spoke again about Ellen, but he decided to keep his thoughts to himself. They were dark thoughts. The notion of ten years passing since he lost his dear wife prompted something inside him to rekindle the hatred he had known some years back. Was it too late to find the man responsible? It might have been accidental, but surely the man who fired recklessly had to face the law – some kind of law? Or should he carry on working hard to forget everything that happened on that fateful day?

I have a name, he thought, *I have a name, and he can be traced.* Maybe, he wondered, I might be able to sleep at nights. He had grown used to his lonesome life, talking to himself and keeping busy with the *Informer*. But if he didn't act now, he never would, and he would never rest easy again. It was such a powerful feeling, this burning need for revenge, that it took his mind off the fact that he and the *Informer* were under threat. It was Kenny again – that name signifying destruction. Kenny wanted the paper, and the offer was too much for his partners to resist. The game was almost up, he thought, but at least he could spend his time looking for Cal Roney.

THREE

It had fallen to Jim Kenny to take charge of the everyday affairs of the ranch. Brothers Eddie and Jake did their bit at times, but it was Jim who saw to the ranch hands and made sure the fencing was done and the growing mass of cattle watched over. On the morning after the escape from the jail, the brothers were together at breakfast, and Eddie, the eldest, was dishing out orders as usual. They were all lithe and gaunt, faces always holding back any particular expression; they inherited their father's animal quickness. He had been dangerous as a rattler and speedy as a spooked deer. The boys were middle height, muscled and eager, with no fat on their bodies and unrest on their faces.

Eddie, in between chewing on biscuits and waiting for Jim to dish up the warmed-up stew, was in no mood to ease off on the locals. In fact he was more determined than ever to grab what was left of

34

Long Corral, the law included.

'Look boys, Stile is the rogue in the pack here – a wolf. We have to cut him out and then take the shirt-and-tie spouters. They'd run from their own shadows, boys!' The brothers enjoyed a laugh at the expense of the more obviously upright members of the town.

'See boys, them Heaths and Stile, they have one plain weakness. They have a moral sense. Right? Now you and me, we don't have that sort of weight on us, and so in any situation, we'll have one over them. Now morality is a fine thing in its place, if it suits an individual. But puttin' morals in the heart of things, why that's asking for a defeat. You've already lost the battle if you got moral scruples.'

Jake said, 'I'm still laughin' at the jail, Eddie. What kind of lawman runs a jail like that? I mean a buck rabbit would be out of there in a wink. We were dug out while Stile went for a whiskey break.'

'He does like a whiskey, that's for sure, and that's another weak spot. This is gonna be easy pickins, brothers dear!' Eddie took some stew now from Jim, and all three tucked in like they were ravenous wolves at the kill.

Jim, feeling left out as usual, had to have his say: 'Look Eddie . . . it's time you gave me something more to do. I mean, I'm the work-horse around here. You think of me with a spade or a hammer . . . not a gun! Give me some more to do!'

'Don't worry, Jim . . . you only have to ask. Just tell me what you want to do!'

'I know precisely what I'd enjoy . . . there's the folks down at Blood Creek. Now we could use that place. We need it real bad, Eddie. I mean they got water and wood, to say nothing of the horses. That old-timer, he rounded up five of 'em. . . . He's one of the best rustlers I ever seen. What do we do about them, Eddie?'

'Now, you're readin' my mind, little brother. I been thinking we could take that place. Just take all three out and use that as a look-out. It's a damned sight closer to the town than our good old Double T.'

'Eddie, let me and the boys do that, eh? I can take Coop and maybe some more men, and we can pick 'em off any time you like.' Jim wanted to impress his big brother and had always wanted to earn his respect.

'What about Coop . . . can he be trusted? He has one leg only half moving and he likes the bottle too much.'

'I'll make sure Coop's sober. He likes to rule the roost, mind. Tends to shout out orders as soon as he sees me. Well, I'm gonna turn that around. . .and I'll find his stash of booze before we go.'

'Let me go and take a look first,' said Eddie, now throwing some coffee to the back of his throat. 'I heard the young one there is handy with a gun. He done a robbery. Got some red blood and a cool head to do that. I'll pay a call and then give you some orders.'

Matt Calero had done what Lerade had asked him to do: he had put a letter on board the Long Corral stage addressed to Macky Heath at his hotel in Long Corral, mentioning that a Pinkerton man might be around town at some point soon, and could he keep in touch with him and report on what was happening? He didn't want to interfere. He knew that Cal was a lone worker, a self-sufficient type who saw others working with him as a risk, a threat to success and security.

Macky had enough to do without worrying about detectives who might in the end be a nuisance. But he replied to the note saying he would watch out for the man and act accordingly. The one thing the note did achieve, though, was to set Macky's mind in a frame to worry about what might be going on. It could be good or bad, he thought. The sheriff of the town was nowhere around, and so what was going on that a detective had to be sent to the area? But he had the contact in Calero, and if there was any trouble he would send a rider to Laramie, for help.

For Macky, it was a sign of his position and favour that the Pinkertons thought of him. It was part of what he and his brother Doc had been working for over the years. Nobody in authority, if there was any problem, ever thought of talking to Eddie Kenny. They came to the Heath brothers. Maybe one day, he thought, as he read the note and considered its importance, maybe one day, the town would be a real, safe, civilized settlement, free of the power-crazy land-grabbers and despots like the Kenny outfit. While there was a line of communication between the Heaths and the Pinkertons, there was hope for something more than just Ben Stile in the fight to preserve the law.

He knew that he was under threat from Eddie Kenny. He knew that Kenny wanted the hotel. He and Doc were up against ruthless individuals and they were a long ride from help if they needed it. But at least someone out there knew his situation. It was a fight against time, he knew. Kenny would run out of patience. They had put him off time and time again, with meeting after meeting and lawyers' letters passing back and forth. Kenny was itching for a solution, and everybody knew it.

Macky had written his reply. Now, in between running the hotel and keeping the singers and musicians happy, he would keep checking on strangers to see if the law was around after all. The only hitch was that there were always strangers, and plenty of them. In fact, he wondered, how was a man to know a Pinkerton detective when he saw one? They surely didn't have a uniform, and they didn't advertise who they were and why they were there. It was a mysterious profession. He had always thought that it said such a lot about the frontier that the representatives of the law and justice had to move by stealth, in disguise, against the forces of anarchy.

Maybe, he thought, a detective is actually the man who looks least like any kind of lawman; maybe he is the scruffiest wastrel that hangs around the cookhouse for scraps and rides a diseased, fly-bitten mule? Whatever he looked like, he was on his way, and a detective was better to have around the place than a tramp or a thief – the types most often blown in with the sagebrush.

It was a bright morning in Long Corral and Ben Stile was catching up on some reports, and expecting a call from Doc Heath and Octavius, who had promised to have some ideas on how to improve the jail. But his mind was still dwelling on the previous day's brush with death, and the problem of the Kenny clan. His mind was telling him that he should go and see how the mysterious stranger was doing, but he needed his eggs and bread and was lingering over the food when the visitors came. The doc walked in first, glanced at the jail wall with the hole in it, and tutted. Behind him, Octavius Gibbs couldn't help laughing.

'Oh Ben, Ben . . . this will never do. You have to

step up, man, and do the job right.'

'Sonny, for God's sake don't write about this in your paper. Stop grinnin' like a weasel in a hen house as well, you're startin' to aggravate me!'

Gibbs sat down by the window, and Doc Heath moved into the open cell and inspected the hole in the floor. 'Ben, how did they get tools? They had to have tools.'

Though keeping quiet about it, the doc was nursing a suspicion that Ben Stile had let the Kenny boys get out. Maybe he turned a blind eye and then put on an act. But that wouldn't have been something Ben Stile would do. He decided to test his friend.

'Ben, I've known you an awful long time. You've always been a sound, reliable lawman. I know that every person in this little town would trust you to do a good job looking after them, but you have to admit, this looks a shade dubious. . . I mean, three rogues diggin' out of a jailhouse! Come on. . . .'

'You insinuatin' I've sold out to Eddie Kenny? That I'm that weak?'

'No, he's not saying that, Ben,' put in Gibbs. 'He's thinking how this story would look if it did get a page in my paper . . . or if word got around, which it won't, I can assure you!'

'Dammit, word has already got around. The folk in this town, they can't tell skunks from house cats and they believe what they see, and think the worst of it. I mean, fact is, I had left the jail . . . just for a short time . . . and they had it all planned. They must have been digging in the nights over the last week or so.'

'Look, forget it for now. Let's just say we need a new jail. This old place is hopeless, Ben. I'll get the citizens together and we'll vote you some cash for this. Right?' This was the doc, and he now held out his hand for Ben to shake it. 'I wasn't insinuating anything, Ben. You're a good man. Truth is, we need to stand together agin the Kenny boys. We all know what they want – the whole town.'

'Yeah, they already bought the two stores, the stables and the saloon up the far bend,' Ben said. 'Where is this all going to stop? I've met his type before. He ignores all rules. You know, he once said to me that the law we all bow down to ain't his law. He said, *my law is the only law, mister.* That's what he said, to my face.'

'They want our place,' the doc added. 'Eddie Kenny has upped his offer this month. I'm fearin' he's likely to lose patience soon and just take the Heath, like he's took everything else he has. I have to remind you, my friends, that his father taught him to grab and deal with the consequences later. But he's worse than old Kenny. Eddie ignores all the consequences!'

Eddie tapped the arms of his two brothers and then

41

looked them in the eye, in turn, before putting a great beam of pleasure on his face and saying, 'You know, boys, everybody between Cheyenne and the Platte is gonna know about the Kenny outfit, and how Pa would be so proud of what we done. Look at him up there . . .'

They all turned to look at the portrait of their father, hanging in pride of place, several feet above eye level. 'Now, get busy . . . I'm paying a call on Blood Creek!' His brothers went, and Eddie stayed there, taking the time to talk to the picture, as he had done so often before.

'Pa, I know you're lookin' down from Heaven and you're thinkin' you're puttin' your spirit here, among us. Well, you might not have rated me much when you was here, but I'm gonna make you proud of me now!' He kissed a finger-end wet and then stretched up so he could dab the finger on his Pa's cheek. 'You didn't notice me, Pa. You never said much, but my love for the Double T and you is gonna be *proved*. See? You was never proud of me in your life, but you will be pretty soon. . . .'

Cal was nervous as he lay there, still being cared for by Emilia and Doc Heath. He was expecting to be recognized at any moment, and the only thing he could think of as soon as he was able to sit up was that he needed some place where he could be alone, and not be seen. When Doc Heath came late at night to check on his patient, Cal was still bound around the head, and the bruises on his face were still swollen. The Cal of ten years back was not there to be identified, but he soon would be, when the healing had worked out.

He asked Emilia to find him a room somewhere. If he could be well enough to ride, he would hightail it out and run to ground until he was well enough to work again. But would she co-operate? The doc agreed that rest and quiet were needed, and he didn't stay long. But Emilia, sitting by his side again, was as worried as Cal about the situation.

'Sooner or later somebody is going to remember who I am,' Cal said, 'What I need is a hole to crawl into, just for a few days. Can you help?'

'Mr Roney, you've just come down from the burning of a fever. You need close attention.'

Cal, when he looked at her, saw the most beautiful woman he had ever set eyes on. Life had given him no time for getting to know women, but this one was special. 'Look, Miss Emilia, is there anywhere at all? Please help me. I'm not the monster you heard about.'

She thought for a moment. Her forehead creased with worry, and he hated to do that to her. 'Mr Roney, there is a room. . . it's used by a landlady here who has rooms for travellers, some inside and one out the back. You could lie up there. I'll come to you. But I have to tell you, I'm not happy about it.'

He wanted to embrace her to show his appreciation, but when he moved up a little the pain was so bad he slumped down again. 'When night falls tonight then, you'll guide me there?' he asked, and she nodded.

'I'll tell them that you left town.' She said, 'But I hate lying. Mr Roney, you're bad for me. . . .'

'Please stop the Mr Roney politeness, Ma'am . . . I'm Cal.'

'You are Mr Roney . . . my patient. Yes, you saved my brother's life, but you are also a reckless gunman, an adventurer. I'll help you till you're well enough to ride out, and then I never want to see you again. You know, Mr Roney, I've heard it said a thousand times, a patient starts to feel smitten with his nurse! Oh yes, that happens all the time. But don't you go thinking like that, because it will not happen here!'

Cal thought that would be very hard to take, but said nothing. He had almost fallen for the fantasy that this was his own woman, caring for him, fussing over him, listening to his talk and soothing his pain. He had seen it in the war, when the wounded were cared for by local women. It was a strong, deep bond, this nurse and patient business. But it was more than that: the more he had time to lie and think of her, the more he imagined being with her, spending most of his days with her – though he knew full well that this was as ridiculous as a boy's

44

imagining being a medieval knight or thinking that the tales in the picture-books were real.

Still, in spite of all that reflecting on this, Emilia was a beautiful woman, and he loved spending time with her. Maybe it didn't have to be a dream?

At Blood Creek, Lizzie was doing the washing in the stream. It was a hot but clear day, and the birdsong was charming her as she worked. The water lapping at her feet was comforting, and she was humming a tune to occupy the time. Cy was out to shoot supper and Sedge was cleaning the house. She was thinking just how much she wanted to stay here, to put down roots. There had been too much running away, too much moving on, in her life with Cy. Wyoming was new country, just finding itself, and it was exciting to be here and to be part of it. She also had some thoughts about maybe writing for the *Long Corral Informer*, and had vowed to talk to Mr Gibbs about that. She had always been a reader, and now wanted to write for a paper, though she would write with a man's name, most likely.

The humming of one of her favourite old songs came to an end as she concentrated on rubbing soap into a stain on one of Cy's shirts, and in that lull she sensed something or someone watching her. Without moving her head or looking across at where she heard the footfall in the dry under-growth, she said, 'Who's there?'

Eddie Kenny stepped out, a broad smile on his face, and he stood, arms akimbo, only ten feet from her. Lizzie pulled a knife from her belt and stood up, then crouched defensively, holding the knife point towards the stranger.

'Who are you? Watching women like that. . . hiding in the scrub . . . that's not what normal, law-abiding folk do. Who are you?'

Eddie put his hands up in the air. 'See, I'm not reaching for a gun. I mean no harm. I'm Eddie Kenny, I run the Double T. You most likely heard of me, Miss . . . and you're a pretty piece, ain't you?'

She could see how tall and strong he was, so the knife stayed pointed at him. But then he took off his gunbelt and threw it well away from him, and sat down. 'Sit down, Ma'am. . . I just want to talk a little. It's a neighbourly call.'

'Good neighbours don't hide and spy on women, mister. I'm not putting the knife down.' Lizzie kept her face fierce and unfriendly.

'Now, I can't prove who I am. You'll have to take that as truth, and believe me. I mean you no harm, beautiful lady!'

'Cut out the compliments, mister . . . I'm a married woman. I heard about these wandering tramps and their wicked ways . . . you're most likely a wandering tramp . . . there could be a dozen more rogues out there, creeping towards us right now. I read about a poor woman attacked and assaulted in her own home, just a day's ride east!'

Eddie Kenny reached out a hand and said, 'Look, put the knife down and shake my hand . . . please?' But the instant his hand stretched out, a bullet whistled past it and slammed into a rock. Eddie darted back and rolled in the dust towards cover, in case another bullet came his way.

In a matter of seconds, Cy stood over him, pointing his rifle barrel down so that it almost tickled Eddie's chin.

'You eager to die today, mister?' Cy asked, 'Now if that is the case, carry on annoying me. Otherwise, explain yourself.'

'He says he's Eddie Kenny,' Lizzie said. 'But I think he's a thieving tramp.'

Eddie looked up now and said his name again. 'I pay a neighbourly call and this is what I get!' He got to his feet and held out a hand. When Cy saw that the man had no gun, he lowered the barrel and walked the visitor towards the house, with some prods from the gun. Lizzie picked up the gunbelt. She found Eddie's horse nearby and led that homewards.

A while later they were all sat in the house, with Sedge offering Eddie some coffee.

'Kenny, hey? Well, everybody knows that name. You do look as though you got money, I'll say that!' Sedge said, shoving the coffee in front of the visitor, who kept up his polite front, smiling and saying nothing but polite words.

'I'm awful sorry I crept up on you, ma'am . . . I was coming to see you all when I heard the singing and I just had to see who it was. . . it was wrong of me to do that. I don't make a habit of scaring women! I really am the boss of the Double T.'

Then he started asking the kind of questions that Cy didn't want to hear, like where had they come from and did they have any plans – and the questions met with no answers that would give information to anyone. So, he didn't count, didn't deserve no explanations? That was about the size of it. Eddie was frustrated, and he finally asked straight out, 'Mister and Mrs whatever you are, you're real concerned about privacy out here. You told me nothin', and so a man might think that you've somethin' to hide!'

'A man might think you could get out and stop blocking out the light from my table, mister,' Sedge said, running his fingers over the Bowie knife he kept handy in his belt.

'The thing is, Mr Kenny, if that's who you are, you're welcome to drink our coffee and talk a little, but we have a peaceful life here, and we like our own company, so you should go now. Take your gunbelt and go annoy some other folks.' Cy said this without a trace of humour. He was in deadly earnest. Eddie Kenny did smile, and stood up, again offering to shake hands, but was refused a response.

'Just go home, mister,' Lizzie said.

When Eddie was riding home he was burning inside with hatred. They had humiliated him. Who the hell were those people? He hated being made to feel small: he hated it like he hated warm beer or cold stew. They would be wiped out, those ragged drifters – wiped out so there was no trace left of them.

FOUR

Octavius Gibbs slammed his fist on the table, and his suited friends seated around the large mahogany table felt their hearts miss a beat. 'No, no. . . we will *not* accept the offer. The paper was established by me, and it stays a Gibbs paper . . .'

'But Octavius, old friend, the other shareholders want to sell. They have offered enough cash up front for the five of us to put our feet up and never work again! How can we resist that. . . what do you say, you men?' This was Sam Dolan, and he looked around at the faces of his partners for a reply. They all made sounds of agreement. 'You only have forty per cent, Sonny . . . you have to listen to the board here,' Dolan said, staring straight at Gibbs, making an appeal to common sense.

'Yeah, you have to see, we're not young any more . . . it's time to hand the thing over to new blood. Mr Holden will be here any time now and he expects an answer, Sonny.' This was another shareholder, the mayor himself, Pat Grisham.

Gibbs got to his feet now and looked around at all the faces staring at him. Once they had been determinedly behind the *Informer*, and it had been wonderful to be part of such a group of ambitious men. But time had gone on and worn them down. He felt it was time to give them one last lecture, in the hope that they would see the folly of their defeat.

'Look, Pat . . . everybody here . . . this is not only a newspaper. It might look like a few sheets of paper and a gathering of small print features. It might look like letters and opinions of folk sounding off, expressing their dissent, but believe me, it's far more. It's the spirit of the frontier! It's in a local newspaper that we may see, clearer than a mountain stream, the preoccupations of the men and women who are making this territory into the enterprising young settlement that it deserves to be. Only seven years ago the law was passed to open up this vast, beautiful country, and your fathers and mothers came out here, not so long back really, in wagons, facing the Arapaho and any number of renegades. . .We're still living in a young, burgeoning place, and it's a land that needs talented men like us. . . age don't matter! It's the fire in your belly that counts, I tell you. If we give in now, we're inviting in the barbarians. That's what they are, this clan, barbarians. I thought you were learned men, men of taste . . . and here you are letting Mammon lead you into a deal with the devil!'

'What's your point, Sonny?' Pat Grisham asked.

'My point is that a periodical is the only way, and the best way, to see and understand the spirit of a society. You know that ever since I created it, the notion in my head was to make some place where ideas could be exchanged . . . basic politics is what it is, but also the spirit of this frontier and these honest, working folk. But there is more to life than bread and whiskey. There are the finer things.'

'But Sonny, it's time for some new blood. I'm seventy years old and I want to put my feet up on the table and dream, smoke a cigar, watch my grandchildren play . . .' This was Pat again, and Gibbs could see that he was speaking for all of them, because they nodded and made supporting noises. 'I'm too old to fret about the finer things, Gibbs. Life has worn us down and . . .'

'Worn you down and made you softer than a blanket in a whorehouse! Fine, then Isaac Holden will come in here, ask us to sign that paper, and you know what's happening then? The Kenny brothers will shut it down and build a new casino. The only business they know is gambling. Their pa was a gambler, a drifter from down the South looking for an easy buck and a fool to rob. Do you want to be more fools they can rob?' As he said all this, Gibbs went red in the face and had to dab off the sweat from his eyes with his handkerchief.

'So, I'm asking you again,' Gibbs pleaded, 'Will you say "No" and keep the paper away from Kenny?'

Before anyone could answer, a very fat man in a dark suit, having the appearance of an undertaker, walked in. In fact he was an undertaker, but he also did some legal work to keep the cash flowing in. 'Isaac Holden at your service, gentlemen!' He laughed as he spoke, as if the whole world entertained him. 'Mind if I rest my body here?' The board kept silent, but Pat told him to make himself comfortable, and he sat on one chair and put his legs up on another. He was what everybody's idea of an undertaker would be, apart from his pleasant disposition: gaunt face, long black coat, and beneath it a suit, shirt and bow tie. In his coat lapel was a freshly picked rose. 'Now, I have the necessary papers.' He opened his bag and brought out several sheets of paper. 'You have received copies of this . . . and you have all read the text, I trust?'

Everyone mumbled their response. They were familiar with the terms.

'Before we discuss the price, Mr Holden,' Sonny asked, 'I would like some reassurance that Mr Kenny will continue the paper and employ an editor.'

Holden was sweating now, and he wiped his brow with a bandanna that had been stuffed into his pocket some time back and never been washed. 'If you read the papers, Sir, you would know that the *Informer* will be discontinued. My clients want to buy the building and everything in it. Now, please would you all sign this sheet?' He slid a sheet of paper on the table and slid it along to the nearest man.

'If you sign this, then you curse this place with more Kenny destruction . . . give them power and they will turn it to destroy you! I'm not signing it.'

'Now Octavius Gibbs, my client Mr Kenny has nothing but good in mind for his town!'

'His town! The damned cheek of the man!' Gibbs felt like kicking the table, but he had to watch the paper circulate, each man signing it and passing it on. 'We need the money, Sonny, sorry . . . we just need the money . . .' Pat said, grimly.

As Holden gathered in the papers and then shook hands with those who had signed, Gibbs stamped out, vowing to see them all in hell, because he would never spend time with them in their town again. 'I'll fight back. . . I got friends!' he yelled. But the others all muttered that Octavius Gibbs had just lost his last few remaining friends.

It didn't take long for him to come up with one last thing he could do, something to stir things up a little out at the Double T. He could print one last issue of the *Informer*. It would be the perfect way to put a rattler in the road the Kenny brood appeared to be riding on. He went straight from the meeting to the *Informer* print shop to see Charlie, his production man. 'Charlie ... we need to throw some mud at the very perdy portrait of our old foe, Kenny. We're doing one last issue of the best paper this side of the Rockies!'

It was dusk when Emilia led Cal across the back road, from the rear door of the Heath Hotel. He had very little to carry, and she brought her medicines and bandages. No one saw them leave, and it was such a quiet yard behind the main buildings that, as they trod carefully and stealthily to the shack, even the dogs didn't sense any movement.

'Now get into that bed and I'll get you some food,' Emilia said, tucking him in. Cal hated the need to be mothered and fussed over, and he was not a good patient. But now, feeling about her as he did, it wasn't so bad, and he didn't have to force a smile when she was there.

'You are surely the kind of sick man that doctors and nurses complain of ... now shut up and take this.' She made him drink a brew that Doc Heath had given her for him.

'When will I get out of this hole? I feel better.' But as he said this he winced in pain as he moved his arm.

'You see, you're not right ... two more days of rest and then we'll see.'

Cal's life had never given him the opportunity to

spend time with what he thought of as a real, fine womanly kind – a wifely kind, in fact. Now he had no choice but to look at her, and he loved the fall of her long dark hair as it lay on his chest as she attended to him. There was the smell of a woman too: her delicate scent, that indefinable presence of a gentle, soft-hearted and caring person. One time, as she reached over him to take hold of a dirty glass, his face was so close to hers that for an instant their eyes looked into each other, and then she moved swiftly away and Cal said, 'Beg pardon, Ma'am . . . but you are a real attractive woman, that's all!'

'You can shift any of that kind of talk right out of your head now, do you hear? I been nursing men for a few years, Mister Roney, and they all get smitten, as I told you, by a nurse's motherly care . . . now you read this, to pass the time!' She picked up a copy of the *Informer* that had been lying around, and dropped it on his face.

'I have no time for flirting with men . . . particularly them with bad reputations . . . such as you, Mister Roney!' She busied herself cleaning and tidying the place, as it had been used as a dump for old tools and furniture, and there was only just room for the single bed, which Cal now filled so well that his feet were dangling out the end of it.

'Now you read that, and I'll be back with some warm food, very soon. I've told the landlady here that I'm using it while my own room is being decorated

... everybody knows that Ben's home is a wreck, in need of some rebuilding, to say the least!'

'Does Ben know he has a sister with all your talents – I mean, does he treat you well?'

'None of your business, Cal Roney ... now read that till I get back.'

There was nothing else to do. Cal was aware that boredom was now the order of the day – two days, in fact. Reading had never troubled him, and he had never troubled books and papers, but now here were some words in print and little else to occupy him so he determined to read on. At first there were articles about petty theft, the need to clean the walkways, the noise at the Silver Bullet, the Kenny saloon up the road. It was clear that the staff of the paper, and the high-minded folk who bought it, had no time for Eddie Kenny. This caught Cal's attention and raised a smile:

Dear Editor,

I write as a concerned citizen of this town: one who has tolerated for too long the extremes of iniquity perpetrated by the customers of the Silver Bullet, and notably by Mr Edward Kenny and his family, the owners, who seem incapable or unwilling to take some kind of legal role in containing the nuisance created by the roisters and drifters who gamble, sing, shout and shoot at the moon almost every night both inside the building and out on the streets when the place closes. I demand that the forces of the law apply themselves to quelling this disturbance, and threaten to shut down this revolting fragment of Gomorrah which has been tolerated here for far too long.

Jeremiah Blake, Blake General Store.

This is very entertaining for a sick man, Cal thought, smiling at an attitude he had met with much too often in the new settlements. It was hardly a matter for the Pinkertons, but more seriously he reflected, no Silver Bullet was the right outfit for any town struggling for a peaceful existence. From what he had heard of the Kenny brothers, though, this Mr Blake had better watch his back.

The paper was a much better provider of entertainment than Cal had thought, and time passed quickly. Emilia was soon back. She had food, but she also had news, and it was news that Cal didn't want to hear. 'Mr Roney, I'm sorry to come back in here with a long face, but my brother has some trouble on hand. Seems his enemies are too restless to give him time. . . .'

'Time for what?'

'Time for walking across to see the world from their point of view. In short, Eddie Kenny sent a

58

messenger to him today – threw a package into the jailhouse, which is all but a ruin, as you know.'

'What kind of package? Something dangerous?'

She pulled a face, showing disgust. 'Mr Roney. . . . It was . . . it was a heart, most likely a steer's heart. And there was a note, which said "*For a coward. Come out in the mornin' if you dare*".'

'I don't even have to ask . . . it was a challenge. They want a gunfight?'

She wiped a tear from her eye. 'Mr Roney, you saved him, but we'll need a regiment to protect him now!'

'I'm heartily sick of hearing the name Kenny! Who do they think they are . . . God's representatives on His earth?'

'No . . . Satan's, Mr Roney. They are Satan's brood, those boys. They've got cash enough to bribe an army and guns enough to supply an army. Their father started a war, and they want to finish it. Before this year's out, I reckon this place will change its name to Kenny Corral. They won't rest until they have the whole town, from roofs to rat-alley.'

Cal had plenty of time to think about the situation of these townsfolk. Never before had he appreciated just how much they were up against. He knew what the weather could do. They were pitted against that, whether it was storms, floods, blizzards, drought and such, but they were facing greedy monsters like Kenny as well. What was worse was this gunfight frame of mind. It was rife wherever a man set down after a journey from back East. In his experience, from Texas to Wyoming, and across from the Goodnight and Loving trail over to Missouri, a man could be called out, sometimes because his reputation was sounded before him, or maybe there had been some cheating at the card table.

Cal had known it. He had moved around in that circuit when he was younger and foolish as a maverick kicking up dust. Sure, he had called a man out. He had been called out. It was all a mindless game, a trial of wills and courage. But for what? For a hollow reputation and a free drink or two when the bucks all patted your back in the saloon.

It was much worse when the man challenged was a lone star such as Ben Stile. The man had courage enough for a regiment. But he stood alone. Cal damned his wound and his bed-ridden state. Something had to be done.

But when Emilia came back in and checked his condition, then wiped his head with a cool wet cloth, he felt the rage ebb away, and the faintness overwhelmed him again.

FIVE

At the Double T, Eddie Kenny was in what the family referred to as his Planning Den. It was a long room with enough wall space to take as many framed pictures as a municipal museum and gallery, and he was proud of it. The Den was the Kenny family history, stretching way back to rural Ireland a century earlier. The Den had been built up into a gallery and a store of all the memories of the family, from their first shack to the wide, powerful establishment it was today. It was all the work of Nathan and his father before him, followed by some help from cousins and friends arriving from their homes back in Ohio, all going out there for a new life and for new riches. He would sometimes walk along past all the drawings and pictures, reminding himself of what the place was like twenty or thirty years back, and then he felt the warm glow of satisfaction as he

61

took his seat again and felt proud, rich and successful.

There they all were, the Kenny ancestors, their
portraits in gilded frames, and every one of them
looking like successful men: suited, bow-tied and
self-satisfied, some smoking cheroots and some
holding fat accounts books. Mixed in with these
were old drawings of the old home in the Emerald
Isle and farmland, all from Galway. They were from
a tough, exposed land, facing the mighty Atlantic,
and when the hunger for adventure and wealth had
led the first men over that great ocean to the New
World, the journey had brought them opportunities
– and that was the watch-word of the Kenny story.

Eddie was thinking about opportunities as he sat
in the huge leather armchair his pa had bought for
use at meetings, so he could head the groups of
enterprising types who worked with and for him. He
was thinking about just how all the plans had been
coming together well, and the day when he and his
brothers could ride into Long Corral and find that
everything their gaze landed on was theirs, and
theirs only. He tore off a broad sheet of paper from
a heap on the desk and drew a rough outline of
what was working out. He drew the main street and
made squares to show the Silver Bullet, then the
Kenny stables, and then opposite was the jailhouse
and court room. That was surely going to be under
their rule very soon. Up the street a-ways was the

grand old building housing the *Informer*, and that was to be the Kenny Casino now. He smiled, feeling the good thrill of satisfaction he was working for, and then drew a rough track representing ten miles, and this led to the settlement at Blood Creek. That was holding out, and didn't seem to have anybody under its roof who might be feeling some fear just now. They were the one big hurdle left. If he had Blood Creek, he had the best route to the north, and the riverside.

There were homesteaders moving in, and they all wanted their patch of land. They would all challenge the herds the Kenny brothers had steadily bought, rustled and hemmed in for many years, and the new arrivals were not to be encouraged. If he had a base at Blood Creek he could easily worry out the new faces and send them back East or further north, though the tribes close by were likely to put the fear of God into the greenhorns trying to learn about cattle or mining.

His mind was sifting all this thinking when there was a knock at the door and in came Jim. He was the tallest and thinnest of the brothers, and also the kid, just making up the numbers. and he had become tired of living with that inferiority. He wore his distinctive black, a colour he had been drawn to ever since he first saw himself as a gunslinger rather than a cowherd. He was red-haired, and the shiny rust hues of hair and beard contrasted sharply with the black shirt, vest and pants. His guns were fancy, the grips carved with his initials, and he had a knife in a sheath rammed through his belt at his back.

'Eddie, I know you're in the Den, and we usually leave you there, but look, I've come to offer to take a little problem off your back.'

'Meaning?'

'Meaning the nuisances at Blood Creek. I told you before . . . now I want to do it. I'll take 'em off the board and out of the game. I know you was down to do it, but you got Stile to attend to, right? So let me and Coop see to the folks out at the Creek. What do ya say? I said before, I can keep him sober.'

'I say Coop is unreliable. First, he's got sixty years on his back, and second, he's too fond of the bottle, not to mention the leg he drags around. He was pa's right-hand man and we've kept him for that. But well, he's nothin' under his hat but hair, and even that is thin as a runt calf. You can see his head's stuck in the past with that damned white Texas Ranger hat . . . he won't part with it, and he's got the damned feather in it so he looks like some kind of Indian fighter.'

'Eddie . . . he's not what you think. He's not drinkin' so much. I can vouch for the man. As for the leg, well he's been dragging that most of his life and he's done fine! What he does have is guts. He don't shrink from any fight.'

64

'You sure, Jimmy? Because we can't easily forget the fiasco at Fuller's Crossing. Damn nearly got me killed. He was unreliable as a steer with a touch of loco root. I've seen infants in school who could shoot better!'

Jim pulled a grimace, as if there was a bad taste in his mouth. 'Aw, look, brother, I'll keep him on the level, I promise. Who is there to take on anyways? I heard there was an old soldier and a sweet young couple more innocent than a babe in the cradle.'

Eddie screwed up his drawing and threw it across the room and into the waste basket. Then he stood up and walked across to Jim.

'Look, Jim, little brother, maybe the time has come for me to trust you. I'll let you take this job, and you can prove yourself. Fine. But promise me one thing: you'll take no whiskey with you. Yes, you're right. There's a young man and a very pretty woman there, fussed over by a lame old man with a tedious sense of chatter. The world wouldn't miss them, you see what I mean?'

Jim beamed with delight and slapped his brother on the shoulder. 'You won't regret this, Eddie. You'll see, you'll be proud of me.' As he walked out he whooped his happiness like a child set free from the schoolroom on a summer's day.

Eddie went to the window and watched his brother walk across to the stables, where Coop was waiting for him, and he saw the two men shake hands. He was thinking he should have let Coop go months back, as he was a liability. But he was Pa's old *compadre* and there was some sentiment involved. The only problem was, that sentiment was like an arrowhead in a wound. You wanted rid of the damned thing, but then you had lived with the wound so long it had stopped hurting.

That morning, sitting up in bed after eating porridge followed by some eggs and bread, Cal was feeling a lot better. The pain had eased a mite, and his head had stopped throbbing with the ache that the crack on the wood had caused. Emilia left him with the food and went to busy herself, working for her brother, but when she returned he was itching to get up and she could see it on his face.

'You're restless, Mr Roney. I know what you want to do. I've seen your type before. You want to take down the scenery in this strange play called life. . . take down the scenery and put on another story because you've no time for this one.'

'I lie to myself, I know, but yeah, I want to get on my feet, dress myself and ride on out of this town, though leavin' you will be sad indeed, nurse Stile! You're the best company I've had in years – since I was billeted with a company of comedians and jokers down South! But now, you know, I could ride a horse . . . I could move around . . . in spite of what you say.'

'Well, forget that. You're not well enough. This is a serious wound you got. I mean, the bullet very nearly caused a bleed we couldn't have stopped. You do see that? All this infatuation with your nurse has softened your brain. If you want to live, then stay as still as a babe in a cot.'

'But you patched me up ... there's a tight bandage on now ... you strapped the pad on ... I can move.'

Emilia gave him a pitiful look and tutted. 'Really, Mr Roney! If you swung a leg over a horse and kicked on out of here, you would bleed again. You understand? I'm losing my temper now, and a nurse should never do that.'

Cal lay back with a sigh of boredom. She had brought some coffee, and she put the cup down on a little table. She saw the paper opened out on the bed and asked if he had read it, and did he want more reading matter?

'Nurse Stile ... words on paper is as tedious as a hot Sunday sermon. But I have to admit, I enjoyed the letters. Folks around here are opinionated all right. You seem to be educatin' everybody so they be contradictory and political. Or maybe Wyoming folk just like a good altercation.'

'Are you a man of politics, Mr Roney?'

'It's about power, and so of course I am. But I'm more a man of justice ... it comes from my own experience. People has to have their just desserts, and a man who has done some wrong has to have a chance to put things right.'

'You referring to what happened here all that time ago?'

'Sure. That was what set my mind on this path today, working for what's right. People forget that I didn't shoot the man facing me . . . I spared the man. I spared Nathan Kenny, but his sons don't see that. I know what they'll be thinking . . . they see only humiliation, Emilia, and I've learned that humiliation is what wounds a man the deepest. He can't take it, and he lashes out. As to the woman that day . . . until my dying day I'll see that woman fall down, full of my lead . . . and I'll see the poor man she left widowed, down on his knees, giving me a look that had more despair in it than a convict's on a scaffold!'

Emilia saw to the pillow and the bedclothes, and then offered her patient more coffee. They both were aware how much he winced in pain as he moved the weight of his body around. 'See?' she said, 'Delicate . . . still in a delicate condition.' She had ignored his comments on the shooting of so long ago, ignoring it because it was too painful to recall and to think about, now that her own brother was in danger of a similar death.

There was a knock on the door, and then a woman's voice was heard shouting Emilia's name. She came in and apologised for disturbing them.

'Emilia... your brother ... he's real het up. I left him cleaning his gun and cursing the sheriff.' She was Meg Carson, and she was what society saw as a poor widow, but in fact she ran her bed and board so well that she was one of the richest people in Long Corral. Meg was nearly fifty, wrapped in a plain blue dress and shawl, and her healthy red face was creased from worry. Her brown hair flicked across her face as she spoke.

'How are you doing, mister?' She saw Cal and heard his moans as she had walked in.

'I'm doing fine ... thanks so much for the use of this place. I wouldn't be welcome here if folk knew who I was ... and I'm aiming to leave tomorrow. You'll soon be rid of me. Now what about Ben ... he's in trouble I guess?'

'Seems there's been somebody calling him out. There are men around here who still think the rule of the bullet is the law.'

Cal made a supreme effort to push himself to the edge of his bed, swung a leg out on to the floor and then forced himself to his feet, but with a yelp as he did so. Emilia went to him and tugged at his shirt sleeve, shouting at him for being stupid, but he replied: 'Just bring my rifle from over there ... I can cover him from inside!'

Both women took hold of him now and carefully pushed him back down into the bed.

'You will do no such thing!' Meg said, sounding

like a schoolma'am.

'My brother needs me, so I'm going out there. Thanks for coming, Meg. You stay right there, mister!' The women left, leaving Cal panting and feeling foolish. But there was a rage in him, a frustration that he was finding very hard to resist.

Gibbs now had Charlie checking through the archives of the *Informer*. They were looking for every accusation about Eddie Kenny, every negative report and every brush he had had with the law or with decent citizens.

'Bring it all out, Charlie, and everything on his pa while you're at it. We're doing a Kenny Special Issue, designed to rouse the nest of snakes out there at the Double T,' Gibbs said, as he made ready for the material. Charlie was only thirty, but had been with the paper for ten years, after knocking on the door one day in search of some work. He was still the thin youth who had arrived, carrying no flesh and immaculately groomed and dressed. He wore sober dark clothes, kept his hair short and his face clear of hair. A stranger seeing him would have thought him a lawyer or something similar. The one thing he wanted more than anything was Emilia Stile as his wife. He had almost asked her once, but had decided to give her some more time to maybe miss him. They had walked out a few times, eaten together and enjoyed a concert. But she was as dedicated to her work as he was to his own.

After an hour, the broad table in the room was stacked with papers. The two men sat down and sifted through them, pulling out the best, the meatiest reports, the ones that showed the dark brutality of the Kenny clan. When Gibbs started writing up the extracts they were going to use, and Charlie made some coffee, they sat there, looked over the copy, and finally Gibbs said, 'This should fill four pages. It's shorter than usual, but it's a farewell paper, and it's going to have some impact, Charlie, believe me!'

It was late afternoon before the frames were filled and the composition of the letters and boxes was done. They were close to print, and at their last coffee break, Gibbs sat back and said, 'Now, Charlie, read me that leader.' Charlie put his long legs up on a chair and read:

Black deeds of the Kenny Men. . . . In saying farewell to its loyal readers, the *Informer* bows out with a reminder of the questionable past of the man who is to run Long Corral, and his deadly inheritance from his father, a man known across the territory as the 'Land Grabber with the Gun'. The Kenny story includes bullying, fraud, robbery, blackmail and assault. Have the good citizens of the place forgotten the accusation of arson that Edward

faced? Or the vicious assault on a visiting businessman at the Heath Hotel last year? The
brothers who escaped from the town jail and
nobody is interested in arresting them? When
will right prevail?

'Excellent!' Octavius Gibbs felt a glow of satisfaction. But as they were enjoying the moment, Charlie
realized that he had not given Gibbs the news he
had received early that morning.

'Hey, Mr Gibbs . . . we've been so busy I forgot to
tell you the news that came this morning . . . our
sheriff ain't coming back! News is that Sheriff Capp
went to Cheyenne and then decided to go back to
Illinois where he's from. He can't face the challenge
here any longer. A letter came on the stage, and I
should have said . . .'

'Oh . . . so there's Ben Stile, on his own, to face
the damned clan out there.'

'Yeah, unless we do somethin', Mr Gibbs,' Charlie
said, with no idea of what exactly two pen-pushers
could possibly do.

Cal, holed up and in pain, had no idea that another
note had arrived from Calero, urged on by Lerade,
who was worrying again. Calero had asked Macky
for news of whether he had heard anything that
might be happening at Blood Creek, or whether the
agent had made contact with him. Macky, of course,

had nothing to report, and sent a brief note to Calero telling him that.

Both Calero and Lerade now felt that something had gone wrong. They met to decide what action should be taken.

'Look, boss, he's so far away he can't get a note to us. It looks like he by-passed the town and went straight out to the Creek. That's my hunch, so that's why we've heard nothing.' Calero was convincing. Still, thought Lerade, for all they knew there could be ten men out there at the Creek, and there was just Cal Roney facing them.

'Two days . . . two days more, Matt, then I want you to go and head for the Creek. I just think it's best to cover each other. . . play safe. I'd do the same for you. It's not just because he's new.'

Calero knew that it was the opposite of what Lerade said. Of course he was thinking that Roney was in trouble and that he should have sent someone else. But Roney knew the land there better than anyone else. What neither of the Pinkerton men knew was that Macky had far more on his mind than watching out for detectives in disguise.

SIX

The newspapermen were so busy at their office, half a mile from the end of town where the Heath Hotel faced the jail, that they had no idea what was happening as they sat back, feeling pleased at their handiwork. They rolled the press and its rumble covered any sound from outside, so they were cocooned in their own workplace, unaware of what Ben Stile was faced with that late afternoon. Charlie, who had been ambitious to follow in Gibbs' footsteps and run a newspaper himself, had brushed aside the disappointment of the paper being bought out, and put all his energy into hitting back in this way at Kenny.

His dream had been to marry Emilia and dig in somewhere with a new homestead, him being a printer and writer, and she being a medicine woman. They were not short of skills to sell. Now he was rethinking, but she was still at the centre of his plans for the future.

Ben had waited all day, after opening the foul parcel the day before, revealing to him the fatty heart of some beast. All he knew was that he would have to face a gun, or guns, on the next day. Sheriff Capp was expected back, and so as the day wore on, and there was no sign of any Kenny riders, he felt that Capp would arrive and join him. But when it turned five, and he sat outside his jailhouse looking east, he saw the dust and heard the sound of horses coming his way. He went back inside and took his Henry rifle from its rack. He had sixteen rounds in it, and he had the advantage of cover. Kenny and his boys would have to come and get him.

But to his surprise, as he watched from his doorway, a gang of around six riders came in, but they all dispersed into the buildings opposite except one man, who rode to the middle of the road, dismounted and tethered his mount across the road, then walked back to stand alone in the afternoon sun and shout Ben Stile's name.

'Just me and you, Stile ... get out here like a man.'

It was Jake Kenny. Ben put down his rifle. In his belt he had his two Remington Army cartridge pistols. He liked the length of the barrel, but they weren't too long for gun-fighting, and he was comfortable with them.

He called out from his doorway, 'Jake ... I

thought our days of playing this dangerous game were over. Your pa nearly died doing this foolhardy gun-play.'

'It ain't playin', Stile . . . get out here or live in shadows like a coward!' Jake shouted.

He would have to face Jake, and everybody knew how much Jake Kenny bruited round the streets that he was slick with a rifle and even more impressive with his six-guns. There he was now, staring at the jail, his hat tipped back and his hands suspended over the holsters.

'Well, Stile, you a man or a weasel? You got the message yesterday, and you ain't run for it, so I guess you're not a complete coward!' There was laughter from across the road. His men were expecting to have a dead deputy in the dry earth before long.

From somewhere behind the main street, out of the shadow, Emilia Stile came running, shouting her brother's name – but two of the Kenny gang went and held her, pulling her back into the shadows. All Ben could hear was her voice yelling his name. 'Don't you dare harm her, Kenny!' He bawled out, his words carrying a rage as well as a threat. It was time to step out and face the man. As he walked into the light, Jake replied, 'We don't hurt women, Stile . . . she's safe.'

'No living thing is safe while you're above the dirt, Kenny. I'm gonna put you under it. Best use for a Kenny I guess, feedin' the vegetation. All you feed now is your greed, your crazy need to run the world. I got news for ya, Jake . . . ya can't run the law.'

'Don't be so stubborn, lawman, you can't win. Admit you're more yeller than a gold bar, throw the gun down, and we'll just blast the jail down to the dust.'

'You talk too much, Jake Kenny.'

Both men fixed their stare on the other's face, watching for the slightest move of a muscle or any shift of an eye. Then Ben Stile caught a dart of white: it was Kenny's two arms going down for the grips of his guns, and Ben drew in the split second that he saw the movement. But there was another gunshot as well. A bullet ripped into one of Kenny's pistols and the man froze in shock. Ben's shots narrowly missed their man as Jake spun around, thinking in that instant that another bullet would hit him, from behind.

There was a ruckus behind, and as a crowd had gathered, everyone looked around to find the source of the shot that had stopped the fight. This only caused even more chaos and confusion. In fact the shot had come from an upstairs window of the general store next to the Heath, and the man who had pulled the trigger was Cal Roney, now dragging himself back to his hideaway along the back alley. Everyone had flocked to the edge of the buildings at ground level to see the fight, and nobody had noticed him arrive or walk away.

As to the gunfight, the crowd now invaded the street and the Kenny boys lost interest in the matter. Ben Stile went back into the jailhouse, and Emilia ran across the street, burst inside after him and hugged him.

That night, so late that most customers had left the Heath, Doc, Gibbs, Charlie and Macky asked Ben to join them. It was, as they were all aware, a meeting of war. Doc provided the drink and the others sat back to listen, as he soon launched into his theme. 'Now Deputy Stile, first thing to say is, well done. Who the hell fired that shot, we don't know, but you were facing the man. You showed the kind of courage that a sheriff has. We all think that, as we now have a vacancy, you should take the job, and we'll have it confirmed by the marshal when we can get him out here.'

Ben looked cautious at first. It was a shock for him. He had doubts, and he expressed them: 'Now, my friends, I can see that we're the ones standing up to the Kenny lot, but it worries me how quiet the rest of the town are. Where are they now? Where were the men who might have helped me today? By the way, who did fire that shot? Do we have vigilantes now?'

'If it was a vigilante, he was a hell of a good shot. . . we're looking for a marksman of the highest quality, folks!' the doc added.

'You don't want the job, then?' Macky asked, ignoring any talk of vigilantes.

At this point Gibbs stood up and paced the room, looking down at his feet ruminatively, chewing something over, and his actions made all the others pay attention to him. It was a successful device for a lecturer, as he had his audience in his hands then, when he finally faced them all and spoke:

'Gentlemen, please leave all this talk behind and let us focus on one thing: Eddie Kenny wants to run this town ... every little corner of it. His father always wanted it, and never did manage it. Now the son is taking on the task. How do we fight this man? Well, we do it by the printed word and by brain-work, not by force of arms. That's my opinion.'

'Oh I see, so we walk up to the Double T and we ask him nicely, that your plan?' Doc Heath said, his sarcasm laid on thick.

'No. Give me some credit for having some brain left ... Charlie and I have been busy, and we have something to show you ... Charlie, show us the advance copy!'

Charlie had the *Informer* ready and he spread it on the table top. The others gathered around and Macky Heath read aloud the words of the leader article. The rest made sounds resembling hungry dogs and cats on the midnight roofs. Then Gibbs waited for a response. It was Ben Stile who, after his laughing died down, said, 'Octavius Gibbs, you've got more heart than me ... if this gets circulated, he'll burn your office to the ground.'

'No, he won't,' said Charlie, 'He won't because *he* owns it! As of yesterday.'

They all sat down, after flicking through the pages of the paper. Gibbs went on, 'So gentlemen, what do you say? This will draw him out and. . . .'

'I say that words alone won't work,' put in Ben Stile, 'Eddie knows only one language – violence. But your paper will be a big help. What we do is draw him out. Yes, he'll come to the office looking for your head, but my view is that only a showdown is likely to beat the man down. He will come to the office, but we'll be waiting ... if each of us here is armed, we'll face him.'

Gibbs would have none of that. 'Ben, do you know how many hands Kenny has up there? No? I'll tell you. He has an army. He has sixty cowherds, two brothers and a few hired killers he's brought in to pick off the toughest opposition. See, he owns the land out there ... legally ... and he knows that he has his lawyer, that Holden animal, who'll bend the law for him – so slowly but surely he will own these streets here, and every building we have. Therefore, what is our only option? I'll tell you. It's to get Eddie behind bars, and for that we need the law – and far more than one sheriff. So start thinking, gentlemen, of how we can do this. How in hell's name can we

80

get a marshal out here who will face the man? Do we get a platoon of troopers?'

'I suggest we go away and think, then meet again,' Charlie said, and that met with agreement.

'In the meantime, we'll stir him up with this paper,' Gibbs added. 'Now, we have evidence of what he's done. That's why you had him behind bars, Ben. But we just don't have the men to round up a small army and bring them all in – and even if we did, we have nowhere to hold 'em.'

'And that's why I can't be your sheriff, boys,' said Ben. 'I need help, lots of it. Maybe an army if you got one hid someplace?'

Everyone mumbled their agreement, and the meeting broke up, with Ben still saying, to everyone in general, who on earth was the man who fired that shot?

In the yard shack, Emilia was dressing Cal's wound again. She had spent an hour calling him a fool and he had been squirming in pain since he got back from his shooting. Now Emilia knew, and no one else. 'Mr Roney, you did a fine thing, but also a stupid thing. I thank you from the bottom of my heart for saving . . . again. . . my dear brother. The truth is, I can't see a bad man in you. I wish I could tell everybody who you really are and what you did today.'

'That's real kind, but as long as I'm here, you're

likely to be in trouble. Nobody must know what you're doing . . . helping a man they all hate.'

She saw that he was comfortable, gave him soup and then more coffee, and gave him something from the doc that would help him sleep. Then she left. Cal thought about reaching out and taking her hand, and then, losing the words he thought he had ready to say to her, he dropped the notion and called himself a fool. He didn't know what he was afraid of, yet something inside held him back.

Cal knew that he needed sleep, but his thoughts were tormenting him that night. In the early hours he woke up, and his mind was so confused that he wasn't clear whether he was in the middle of a bad dream or just remembering – but in his thoughts he relived the day that Don Lerade had called him in to the Pinkerton office in Laramie and told him about the job out where the Platte bends south a little. It was a long way off, but Lerade knew that Cal was acquainted with that part of the territory. He saw the scene in his mind, clear as day.

'I hear you know that Creek well, out past Long Corral?'

'Sure do, Mister Lerade, I grew up around forty miles north.'

'Well, we're pretty sure that the robber is holed in around that place . . . Cy Felder. He's a desperate man, and he was willing to take a life for a few hundred dollars. He's likely to do it again. Word is he's a bad character . . . willing to steal a coin from a corpse's eyes. Can you bring him in, Cal?'

'Sure. Give me some descriptions.'

'Seems he's close to a veteran named Gulley, survived the war and learned a heap o' bad habits in the process.'

That had been imprinted in his mind, and Cal knew as he came round at sun-up, that he should be out there looking for Felder and Gulley, not lying around in bed. The pain seemed to have eased. His appaloosa was in the stables next door, along with his saddle and leathers, and his guns were hung on the wall in front of him. 'It's time to bring in your man,' he said to himself – but at that moment, in came Emilia, seeing that her patient was stirring, and already mad at him.

'Mr Roney, stay right where you are. I got some pills here for you, and I need to change that dressing.'

He would bide his time, Cal thought, and he cooperated. He sat on the edge of the bed where there was more light, and Emilia started to take off the old bandage. 'Say, Mr Roney, as you saved my brother's life twice now, I ought to know more about you. Where are you from?'

'Truth is Miss Stile, I was reared not too far from here.'

'And your parents?'

She saw from his face that she had touched a

nerve. A flash of pain crossed his face, and she could see in his eyes that there was something troubling him, deep down somewhere.

'They were killed, Miss Stile. I was just ten.'

'Killed? Who did it?'

'I'd call 'em tramps. My family were settled, homesteaders trying to put down roots, but of course, back then there was not so much strength in numbers. Seemed like every day some kind of unwelcome stranger would come into the place. Some wanted a night in the barn, some wanted water and a hunk of bread. . . some preached the Lord at us. But there were rabblin' wild tramps at times, bunches of drifters crawlin' around like rats, after anything, any kind of mischief. One day they happened on our place. It's not a story to repeat to a woman, Miss Stile.'

'I'm stronger than I look, Mr Roney. It helps to unburden these things.' She started wrapping the new bandage around the fresh pad she had brought in and pressed on the wound. It gave him time to think, and he went on, 'I saw it, Miss Stile, I hid and saw what they did. There was one man . . . the leader I think . . . tall man with a real tanned face and a white hat with a feather in it. One of his legs was injured, I saw he couldn't move it too well. Miss Stile, he put a knife in my father's heart while Ma watched. Then she was taken . . . she was taken . . . into another room. I heard screams. I wanted to rush out. I covered my ears. I couldn't take it . . . I ran out of a back door and didn't stop till our home was out of sight.'

She had stopped working now and was looking into her patient's eyes, seeing the deep hurt in there, pushed down in the dark self, the hidden self, of a brave man.

'Life kicked you in the guts pretty early on, Mr Roney.'

'You could call me Cal.' He didn't smile. She let the words pass and told him to lie back. She brought coffee and gave him tablets. 'One more day's rest and you can move around,' she said.

The door opened and Meg looked in, 'Miss Emilia, there's Charlie looking for you.'

Cal had heard no mention of Charlie, and so he risked a personal question. 'He your young man, then, Miss?'

'He'd like to be. Well, he kinda is . . . we walked out. He has asked the question.'

'Asked the question? Course, as you said, you have no time for men. I see.'

'Mr Roney, you don't see anything. Rest now. I'll be back in a few hours.'

'I should be in Blood Creek!' he said, 'Not rotting in here.'

She went out, chatting to Meg on the way, but her tone of voice didn't seem too happy. Maybe, thought Cal, she was one of them women that just don't need a man around.

His mind was busy, planning what was going to happen that day. He could see in his mind the way out, and so he first forced himself across the room, dressed and put on his gunbelt. His arm hurt when he moved it, as it had done the day before, when he pressed the stock of his rifle with it; but pain fades, he found, if you refuse to acknowledge it. Next was the effort of creeping out of the door, looking around like a rabbit sensing a wolf, and out into the yard. He ducked into the stables and squatted down behind some hay bales. It all seemed quiet, except for a smith shoeing a horse over in the far corner. Then there was his mare, Bella.

Cal crept across to her, whispered and patted her neck, then saw the saddle. He needed Bella to be silent as midnight in Sleepyville, and she seemed to sense his needs. Lifting the saddle was so painful he had to stifle a moan, even though it was a Texas saddle, but in a few minutes everything was fastened up and his work spurs, thankfully with no jingle, were slotted into the latigo, where he had secured them a few days back. The next thing was to walk out, real slow and steady, not even disturbing a shred of straw. Bella knew his every click and whisper, and soon they were riding south-west slow as a trot in a park on a quiet Sunday. Every stride gave him a sharp jab of pain in his arm and chest. But at least he was on the move.

After five minutes, there was the open road and the beautiful expanse of Wyoming before him. Soon he would hear the Platte, but first he took in the distant Medicine Bow Mountains, whose foothills had the streams where as a boy he would fish for trout and listen for the calls of the mountain lions. He was nearing the northern tip of Blood Creek, and he decided to rest a while, take a drink, and decide on how to approach the place. He had no idea how many men might be with Cy Felder, and as he was not exactly in full control of his power and strength, Cal was cautious in everything he did.

He decided to walk steadily towards the Creek, which was around five hundred yards ahead. He took his rifle, just to feel secure, and managed to scramble on to a high rock where he could see upstream. There in the distance he could make out a couple of shacks. It was a sight that brought back so much of the affection he felt for this country, going back to his years growing up. After his parents' deaths, he was taken in by an aunt in Cheyenne, and as he looked towards the horizon, following the flow of the creek, he was reminded of that time. The memories of creeping back to the family home once the shooting and the screams had stopped, came to him now.

He had stealthily stepped back towards the house, walked along the back wall and peeped around to see who was there, and his eyes met the

look of his aunt and her brother. She had screamed
and whooped with delight that he was alive, as the
people coming out to see the state of the place after
the attack expected nothing but corpses. He had
been held close to his aunt's chest and then taken
to her home, to the accompaniment of a constant
stream of affectionate and comforting words.

Now here he was, close to that home, about to
arrive at another homestead and arrest a bank
robber. Please let him be alone, he thought.
Though he expected to see Gulley. After the determined efforts to move, ride and be free of Long
Corral, now exhaustion was setting in, and he felt a
weakness overtake him. A voice inside him, a voice
of caution, advised him to sleep out there, where he
was, and move to the Blood Creek homestead early
the next day, taking the inhabitants by surprise. He
would have to scout though, to be sure that Cy
Felder was there.

He waited for the late afternoon to turn towards
dusk before he prepared to bed down. Bella was
happy to rest under a cottonwood tree in some
shade and chew on some grass, along with the feed
he had loaded to the rear ties. There was a useful
half-bow of rocks a little higher than his head, and
in the heart of this he set his saddle down. But he
had nothing to eat, and it was a long old night
ahead, he knew that.

As the rays of the sun were just warming his

boots, Cal heard voices. Someone was up and about real early. He slithered to the rock nearest the creek and pulled himself to the top where he could see the road from Long Corral. Surprised though, he saw two riders come over the rough track that met the road from the north – and like him, they stopped to take a look along the creek. Cal's luck was in, as they moved a little closer to him, and he saw that there was a thin, youngish man and a shorter, stocky man. The smaller one was swigging from a bottle, while the younger one was acting like somebody stole his rudder. He wasn't at all pleased with the man drinking and laughing.

'Coop, I told you . . . throw away the whiskey . . . you've had enough!'

'Now Jim, you know a little drink steadies the hands and fixes the mind on the job in hand. I always did better with some liquor in me. Stop bein' such a cussed preacher-man. Who we gotta face? An old man and a coward runnin' away from trouble!'

'Coop, there could be ten of 'em up there!'

'Now Jim Kenny, your brother said to trust the advice of an older and wiser man, right? Well, I'm ancient. I been workin' for Kenny folk most of my life!'

'I can't see no wisdom anywhere . . . just an old drunk!'

Cal heard the name 'Kenny', and in a second he knew what the situation was. These two were chasing the same man he was. The whole world wanted Cy Felder, but he, Cal Roney, would get there first.

SEVEN

Emilia was with Charlie when Meg brought the news that Cal had gone. Charlie was concerned about his job, but more worried about his life, now that copies of the last *Informer* had been printed and had started circulation. It didn't take long for word to get around, even if folk had not actually read a piece: they would hear about any kind of news and act on that rumour as quickly as they would step out the door.

Charlie had come to Emilia to let her know the situation, and that he was now unemployed and looking for work. They were on friendly terms, in her mind not unlike brother and sister, and he sensed that was the case, so he was burning to find a way to change things, and open up a chance to try a proposal again.

When Meg brought the news, Emilia saw that she had to go straight to her brother and come clean about what she had been doing. Now that Cal was gone, she could spread the news about him. But she knew that it would be unwelcome news, and so she took the chance to have support, and talked Charlie into backing her up. It was a struggle. When she first broached the subject, he responded as everybody responded to the name of Cal Roney.

'What? Cal Roney? Isn't that the man who killed Mr Gibbs's lady wife?'

'Charlie, if you have any feelings for me, believe me when I say that Roney is not the man this town thinks he is. The death of Mrs Gibbs was entirely accidental.'

'Tell that to Mr Gibbs!'

But they went to the jailhouse and there was Ben, who had been expecting a second attack since the aborted gunfight. He had been busy shoring up the walls and reinforcing the window frames. When his sister and Charlie arrived he was anxious. She could see that he couldn't sit still. He explained that it was eatin' him, this expectation that Kenny would come back. 'He'll be here, and this time, I reckon he'll be ready to stop whoever helped me last time. He's no fool, and he wants me out of this office and preferably in the graveyard under six feet of dust.'

'Ben, Ben, listen to me,' Emilia said soothingly, as her brother sat at his table, checking his pistol, swinging the chamber round and wondering who else might come through his door.

'Emilia, you shouldn't be here. You know what the threat is here. You need to be gone – and you, Charlie. You ain't no fighter. Get back to your press.'

'There is no press, Ben . . . but I see you've read our last edition?'

'I have, and it's damned foolish. You're provoking a sleeping lion there, you and your fool of a boss.'

Emilia was struggling to grab her brother's attention, and finally she had to put a hand on his chin, hold his face still and say, 'Ben, I know who saved you yesterday, you hear? It was Cal Roney!'

'Cal Roney? You're saying Roney was here? . . . and, and . . . that he fired that shot?'

'Listen, brother of mine, and listen good: Cal Roney has saved your life twice in the last week . . . he was the man who jumped from the horse! You have looked into his face and not recognized him.'

Ben Stile's jaw had dropped in astonishment. 'Well, I ain't been so stuck for words since . . . well, since you turned down this young man standing here! You mean to say that. . . ? Oh, I see, he was your patient . . . the man you . . . hell, where is he now?'

Emilia was unsure whether Ben was planning to shoot Cal Roney or to shake his hand. She could see by his face that mixed emotions were battling for his attitude to the news. He tried to find some words, but failed twice to make any sense.

'Ben, it's the truth. He was my patient. He told me all about the past. . . you know he didn't mean to kill Mrs Gibbs, don't you? Be honest.'

'Tell that to Octavius. Sonny Gibbs will not change his mind about his wife's death. He's been brooding on revenge ever since Roney walked out of that courtroom.'

'Yes, but I'm asking you, Ben. Is Roney a murderer?'

Ben thought for a minute, then looked her in the eye and said, 'No, course not. It was crossfire. But sister, I swore I would help Gibbs if ever we got the chance to do anything and I said I would do what the law failed to do . . .'

Charlie cut in then, 'Are you saying, Mr Stile, that you are above the law?'

'I'm saying that sometimes a man has to make up for the law's shortcomings. . . Roney was reckless, and the same applies to any man who has no care with his weapons. . . but hell, if Kenny finds out that Roney's here. . . I mean, most of Wyoming wants the man dead. Roney killed one of the Kenny hands that day. The Kenny boys, if they find out who he is, they'll tear him apart. Then there's Gibbs. . . Sonny Gibbs will be loading his gun if he's found out . . .'

Both Emilia and Charlie assured Ben that nobody else in town knew about Roney. 'The three of us here, Ben . . . only we know.' As she said this,

Emilia suddenly recalled what Cal had said that morning. 'Oh God! He said he was going to Blood Creek. Why would he go there?'

'Makes no sense,' added Ben, 'There's just that young couple out there, and their uncle, the soldier with the wooden leg. Why would he be going there?'

'Not just to share a coffee and some memories,' Emilia said. 'He's from this place, Ben ... a way along the river ...'

Ben knew, and he told the tale of the massacre at the Roney homestead. 'I've known that for years, of course... we all know that's why young Roney turned out a rebel. His aunt tried her best with him, school an' all ... but he went bad. He was always a handful of trouble, that boy ... and now he's saved my skin twice! Who would believe that, sister?'

'Your words do not describe the patient I've had in my care, Ben. People change. Even you, maybe?'

Charlie was standing there, wondering how he could help, and when Ben said the only way to find out what was going on was to ride to Blood Creek, Charlie offered to go, and so Emilia followed. 'What? Ride with a woman and a pen-pusher? Charlie, stay here and take care of my sister.'

'You'll have to stop me, Ben,' Charlie said, defiantly, 'I want to be there, and you'll need your sister if you're hurt. I don't want her to go either, but it makes sense to have her along.' Charlie's argument made sense, though his instinct was for his woman to stay safe.

It had now occurred to Ben Stile that if the true identity of the man who had taken the bullet for him was to be known, then Gibbs would be after him, Eddie Kenny would aim to gun him down, and after that the whole town would want him punished, because his name was etched into the memory of them all, and what he had done way back in the dead years was now so much a piece of history that time had judged him and found him guilty.

Out at the Double T, Eddie Kenny and Jake were in the Den and they had plenty to talk about. Eddie was feeling more and more like the general out in the field, applying some tactics in his own theatre of war, which was now stretching from the Platte at its western bend across to Long Corral. But he was now acknowledging that there was something else, or somebody else, at work against him. Whoever had saved Ben's hide had been one hell of a shot, and Jake was worried about that. It was nagging him that maybe the people in Long Corral had brought in a couple of real shooters, professionals.

'Eddie, who could it have been . . . the shooter? There's nobody in that town supports old Ben Stile. His own sheriff has run off with his legs quaking, right? So who fired that damned shot? It was inches from shattering my hand! The bullet smashed into my revolver and it almost broke my finger. It's sore as a chapped backside, and I want to know what we're up against.'

'Now cool off, brother. I told you the direct way was the best,' Eddie responded, 'We go back and we take him with the entire jail . . . dynamite, boy, dynamite!' He was thinking about little brother Jim out at Blood Creek, and how that should be resolved by sun-down. Then there was the matter of the hotel, and that was the day's other target.

Eddie carried on, 'Now, Jakey, to the main business. Every night except Sunday the paperman and his Heath partners get together for a card game or two in the back room of the Heath. Now, first, Gibbs is right now makin' me boil. We buy his paper, and look what he does . . .' He took the *Informer* from the table and tossed it across to Jake.

'This is some kinda crime, Eddie! He's telling lies about us. There's a legal type of word about this . . . great big lies, I reckon. Take him to court. He's even lyin' about Pa, from years back. Who does this fat man think he is? He's as ugly as a burnt boot and he thinks he's somebody!'

'Jake, goin' to court is too dark tie and smart coat for me. No, he's your responsibility. There's this card game, right? Now, you're gonna disturb the game by shootin' some lead into Gibbs's fat head. The only thing is, we need to wait for the jailhouse business. We can't do both in one afternoon. What would Pa do?'

Jake looked up at the portrait of his father and said, 'Take care of the writer man tonight, then the jail first thing tomorrow. But no, I reckon we do the blast and then I'll take care of the Heath idiot who stands in our way.'

'Sure. You got the boys to do that sign yet? I want it ready by the end of the week. Kenny Corral is a much better name for the place. I want that up at the road end, you understand, brother?'

'Yes, as you say. We're doin' it now.'

'Fine. In a few days' time, this will all be done, and we'll have a little celebration, with the sign there, telling the world that it's Kenny territory and that we kick around the others, the little folk, right? Get to it, Jake.'

Eddie was left alone with his thoughts, and he was bothered by just one thing: the Heath brothers and their hotel. It was a fine place. Ideally, he would like them to run it for him. They needed to be on his side. They were not on his list of dead men. The question was, how to keep them as his workers, not his enemies? Shooting dead their friend Gibbs was the way to train them. So they would have to stay, but by fear. He was skilled at manufacturing that. Fear, he often told himself, came out of the Double T as successfully as the steers heading for the buyers hungry for meat and profits.

It was time to do what he did best: send a threat their way, plant some fear in their hearts, down to their bones. The best threat was to know that they had watched their friend die and to reflect that they might be next in line for a casket.

After watching Jim and Coop dithering and worrying about the effects of drink, and aware that these two were heading for the homestead with aims that were far from benevolent, Cal gave Bella a dig in the sides and headed for the man he was supposed to be arresting: Cy Felder. His mind had been off that subject for a while, but now he was trying to concentrate on the reason why he was out there in the first place. There was a robber to be brought to trial. Likelihood was that he was holed up in this place with some like-minded criminals, and they wouldn't ask before they shot at you. The trick was to play a waiting game, to watch and learn, then strike.

When he came near the house, he was heard, and it was Sedge Gulley who came out to greet him. Cal noticed the halting walk of the older man. He had decided to play his hand indirectly, and not to burst in, announcing he was the law, and that he was there for Cy Felder.

'Now stranger, who am I seeing here?' Sedge asked.

Cal pulled up and offered a smile, coming over

real friendly and easy. 'You're looking at a weary rider, on his way to Casper. I could use some chow if you could be so kind.'

From behind Sedge came Lizzie, and she heard Cal's words. 'Now mister, course we can feed you . . . come on in. We were dishing out breakfast.'

In no time Cal was sitting down with all three of them in the house, and Cy had shaken his hand. Naturally they had seen his bandage, and the bruise on his forehead, and he was soon explaining that. 'Oh, I ran into a man who wanted to take my horse. We had a confrontation.'

'You got some medical skills, mister . . . what was your name?' Cy asked, always wary.

Cal had his false name ready, as he did before, 'William Boldwood, heading for Casper, looking for work. I been on the drives and I'm looking to settle into something that does not involve fussing over steers night and day and sweating so I live with a rash and a burning throat.'

They laughed at that, and Sedge recognized the real thing. 'You speak from experience, Mr Boldwood. I was cook for many a drive, and I know the life well.' Cal complimented him on his cooking – and everything was going to plan. They believed him. Cal was biding his time, deciding on how to do the arrest. Meanwhile, there was Lizzie, and she would capture any man's heart, he thought. She and Cy held hands during their breakfast, and they spoke and acted like a happy married pair, talking about the day's work. Cal decided to pry a little.

'Mr Felder, you aiming to stay here?'

'We came here, just wed, aiming to go further, maybe Montana, but we like this place. It's a new start for us. To tell true, Mr Boldwood, we had a hard time of it when we started out . . . poor and sick. It's been hard, but then it's the same for all of us. That was the notion we had, but it's getting hot around these parts.'

Cal was struck by this, and also when Lizzie put her arm around Cy and said, 'This man has been a wonderful husband, I have to tell you. He would do anything for me, and for our dear friend, Sedge, hey, our beloved cook?' She playfully kicked Sedge's legs under the table, and he laughed. Cy changed his attitude a little, as if he thought Lizzie was saying too much. But Cal pushed a little harder, disguising his curiosity under the pretence of innocence: 'Well, I never had a wife, but I wouldn't want to see her go short. Money greases the wheels of matrimony, my aunt used to say!'

They laughed again. Sedge told Cal that he had the right attitude. 'Best of luck in Casper, Mr Boldwood.' As he stood up to shake his hand and then get back to work outside, Lizzie said, 'Say, you're not in a rush to leave, are you Mr Boldwood? You could stay in the little barn. Do you think, Cy?'

Cy looked doubtful at first, but then softened and

agreed. 'Yeah. Why don't you do that, and to earn your keep you could help around here – but then I think you're looking a bit sick with that wound there.'

'He can help me in the kitchen,' Sedge said, 'Lizzie can help with the fence. In fact Mr Boldwood, you know, my life as a cook on the trails made me quite a medical man. Oh yeah, a cookie has to have treatments ready for the results of his food when we have belly aches!' He laughed at his own joke. 'Seriously, Mr Boldwood, I do have something to help with the wound you got under that wrap. How about it? I'll tend your wound, and you help with cooking dinner?'

It was the perfect opportunity for Cal to stay and watch them a while before he made his move. Sedge knew a lot about treating wounds. Over the years, as a trail cook, he had picked up any number of remedies, as cowboys were notorious for their injuries, diseases and general complaints. Sedge was as useful as a medical man for most ailments.

Cy was not entirely satisfied, and felt a shiver of suspicion about the visitor, but said nothing to Lizzie. They got to work on some timber, both working a saw at first, but Lizzie's eyes kept going to the road. When she heard cracks and breaks in the undergrowth up the slope towards the house, she decided to open up. 'Cy, we need to get back to the house. . . I saw some men on the road. . . maybe they're after something ... come on!' No sooner had they taken a few steps than shots rang out and bullets bit the dust a few feet from them. They went down into cover.

The shots had alarmed Cal and Sedge, and Sedge had grabbed his rifle and squatted by the window, while Cal went for his pistols, pulling them out ready for action before he sat beside Sedge. 'I left my rifle in my saddle,' Cal said, 'Out there in your stable with my horse.'

Out in the cover of the cottonwood trees, Jim and Coop were not agreeing too well on what to do. Jim had wanted to steal into the nearest building and wait for a victim, but Coop was for an all-out attack.

'Now, kid, that's the way I always did it. That's how your pa and me went about things, see?'

'I promised Eddie we would take the place. I promised we would make some bodies and bury them. Problem over. Now look at us, standing here in the open, with at least two gunmen in that shack over there.'

Before they could utter another word, a shot rang out and a bullet chipped the bark next to Jim's head. They both scrambled down into the earth where they crawled like reptiles. 'That's three gunmen, Coop. How many more do you reckon?' He was given no answer. Coop just tipped up the front of his hat and gave an almost toothless smile. 'Let's just rush the place, Jim!'

'No. We wait till dark. This has to be a slow job, now.' They moved back and took deeper cover, and as they settled, they saw two figures move like jack rabbits across from the scrub to the shack, in a split second.

'That's four gunmen, Coop. Are we staying?' Jim's willpower was weakening.

Inside the shack, the defenders crouched around a corner, sitting on the floor. Sedge, speaking from wide experience, asked the obvious question, and then answered it. 'What do we do now, folks? I say we sit this out, and make them nervous.'

It was natural for Cal to take charge. He had always done that, way back to his army days, and on the trails. As a Pinkerton man keeping his cover, he played a role to some extent, but the commander came through. 'Look, first, who could they be out there?'

Cy had his answer ready. 'Mr Boldwood, I need to tell you this . . . the law is after me. I robbed a bank. It was a very foolish thing to do, but we were desperate. Lizzie and me hadn't eaten for three days and beggin' achieved nothin'. I know that's wrong. But the fact is I stole a few hundred bucks and the bankers back in Cheyenne and Laramie, they joined up and I'd guess they got the Pinkertons on my trail. Out there, my money's on them being two detectives.

104

'And you know what,' Cy went on, 'I heard when I was in town that there's a curse on this place . . . a hex. Story is that a man went loco here and slaughtered everything he loved. His mind went so mad he was bitin' himself. That's why it had its name. He threw the corpses in the water and then shot himself in the head. That's what I heard. He was called Cary. But I came here anyways, 'cause I didn't believe that old wives' tale . . . but you know what? I'm wonderin' about it now!'

'They're just two rustlers taking a chance,' Lizzie said.

Cal's brain was working overtime, and he almost broke into a sardonic laugh with the irony of his position. He didn't want to admit it, but his heart was softening towards these two young people. 'Look,' he said, 'I was told about this place when I was a kid . . . I know about Cary and his island. My pa told me there was a curse. It all stemmed from Cary, holed up in there, wanting to be alone.'

The more Cal looked at the married couple, the more he thought about Emilia. Women had never figured in his life because he had never made room for them. But his time being nursed had forced him to look at a beautiful woman, to get to know her a little, and he was now sensing that he wanted to be with her. Strangely, Sedge, who was a wise and perceptive man, was conscious of something in Cal because he asked him, 'So you grew up not far from here . . . did you settle here, have a family?'

'No Sir, I've always been on my own. Lonesome but not lonely, I guess. The war and the trails filled my life and then, wham . . . it's all gone and I'm going grey!'

'What about a woman then? Have you had a special woman?'

There was an uneasy silence. Nobody had ever asked Cal that before. Nobody had ever asked him about women. 'Now, Sedge, as I understand it, a woman fills your life up. She asks a lot. I've never been a giver. That's my fault, I guess. My own self filled up my time.'

'Same thing for me, partner!' Sedge laughed and put out his hand, and the two men shared something important.

'Now,' Cal asked, 'Do we just wait?'

'Only thing is,' put in Sedge, 'We have to sit on this damned hard floor for hours. . . .'

'No' Cal said, 'There's no need. I'm goin' out to circle the shooters.'

Sedge pulled a face and screwed up his forehead into a frown. 'You're still in a fragile state from the stitches what some doc put on you there, son. I say we stay put. Come the night, one of us could do that then.'

Cy was more edgy than anyone else, and he expected the worst. 'Look, they are Pinkertons, and they will be expectin' reinforcements any time.

Maybe there's another and he's ridin' off for help right now! We gotta act fast, Sedge. Boldwood, you're right. Hitting hard and fast wins the day. I never heard of Pinkertons being outsmarted, but they could be outgunned.'

Sedge was all for encouraging Cy to go, and the young man made ready, checking his guns, but Cal could not go along with that. 'No, no, Cy. I have no wife, no kids. I'm the one to go. Sedge, your leg's bound to slow you down, though I know your heart's strong as an ox. I'll crawl round behind them and pick 'em off.'

Cy was starting to think that the drifter looking for work was not what he seemed. He was too capable, too committed to action. Was he a hothead on the loose, or was he a wanted man? He sure acted like an army officer. But they let Cal go. They waited some hours, for when dusk was filling the air. Then Cal took Cy's rifle and went out the back door, on his belly, real slow. There was a thick line of vegetation ahead of him, and a pile of old logs. He would make that his first vantage point. Slow as a snake with a rat in him, he slithered across to the wood and squat down.

Inside, Sedge, Cy and Lizzie managed to drag tables and chairs across to the window to block any light and to hide behind. It had been quiet out there for hours, so they were expecting trouble now. Everybody had been patient, but now Jim Kenny was restless. He bawled out, 'You in there . . . we just want you gone. This is Jim Kenny . . . we want you out. This is a Kenny place and we got deeds, from a lawyer, Mr Holden, you hear? Mr Holden, a real lawyer. Now you leave . . . come out with your hands up, and you can ride away.'

'Jim Kenny, this is my land. You're trespassin',' shouted Cy.

As Jim was talking, Cal knew he wasn't figuring to shoot at him, so he moved as fast as he could, his mind overcoming the pain, to where he could see Jim Kenny. He and Coop were on their knees, behind a thick shrub, their rifles pointed at the window, where some shadows could be seen moving. He could see Jim Kenny clearly and he raised his rifle, ready to aim at the head. But in that instant, in the fading light as some late sun was directed at Coop, Cal saw a man whose very presence made his heart miss a beat. His jaw dropped and his gun fell down to the dust, because in that beam of light he could see the hat with the white feather, and once again he was the terrified little boy, seeing his father die.

He saw that his dropping the rifle had made a sound, and both men glanced across to where he was. In a panic, Cal shot at Jim, and the bullet ripped into his right arm. He went down with a shriek. 'Coop,' he called, 'Coop, we need to go and get help!'

Cal saw the white-hatted man get to his feet and start to walk, wrapping an arm around Kenny, as they both staggered out of the line of fire. He dragged one leg as he moved, as if the limb was only half functioning. There was no doubt in his mind now that the man he had heard called Coop was the man who had killed his father. He started after them, as quickly as he could, and he saw that Kenny slipped and fell again, clutching his arm. White Hat looked back, saw Cal raise his gun, and in that second, he saw and knew Cal.

'I'll be damned ... Cal Roney! You a ghost?' Coop said, firing a shot to stop Cal making any progress, and then he moved on into the darkness, shouting, 'I'll be back for you, Jim!'

A short while later, Cal stood over Jim Kenny, who was whimpering and holding his arm. 'You'll pay for this, mister,' he whined.

'Unlikely, mister. I have nothin' in my pocket book!'

'I was talking about paying with your life.'

'I know that, but you see, the big war didn't kill me, and the tribes on the Plains didn't kill me, and damn me if the heat and flies didn't kill me, so your brother will have to be somethin' real exceptional!' Cal chuckled with delight and Jim Kenny hated him for it.

'I heard you was a gunslinger, Roney? I heard you could have killed my pa. Why didn't you do it?' Jim

109

asked, puzzled.

'You know, young Kenny, you need to exercise the brain in there. . . takin' a life is not always the right way, and it's not always as easy as you might think. Sure, you can pull a trigger. But you are takin' a man's life, and that's big. It is in most folks' minds, though I'm startin' to see that a Kenny has no scruples in this matter.'

'Well, you didn't kill Pa. Clearly, you are a gunman to be respected, I have to say. Though I'm fast losin' any kind of fellow-feeling for you after what you done today.'

Cal grabbed hold of Jim Kenny by the collar and lifted him off the ground. He found enough strength, though agonizing pain shot across his chest where muscle touched the wound, and he slammed the kid against a tree trunk. 'Kenny, you got a lot to learn. Most of all, you got to learn that life is valuable. . . a life is worth something, and it's not counted in gold or silver. You follow me?'

He held the youth so firm and tight that he whimpered and his face creased with the spasms of pain that went through him. 'Yes . . . I understand . . . put me down, you madman!'

'Sure. Respect for life, you see. . . even the life of a sewer rat like you!' Cal dropped him back to the earth with a thump, and the kid moaned and whined like a stuck pig.

110

EIGHT

Matt Calero was riding out towards the south, with the Medicine Bow heights on the far horizon, thinking that it would take a couple of days to reach anywhere near Blood Creek. He had decided that Lerade was nothing more than a worrier, and would fret over red wine spilt on a rug. Cal Roney could take care of himself, he was sure. This was a perfect time to go steadily, easily, take in some free time out in the open. He had been shut inside sitting at a desk ever since the fight at Dentstown six months back.

He was convinced that there was no emergency, no massacre, and certainly no ghost or witch awaiting him out at the Creek. Consequently this gave him a couple of days in which he could take in the beauty of the land, do a little hunting and shooting, and maybe, when he reached the place, sink a few drops of the gargle varnish with good old Cal, who was a loner like himself.

But he did have a secret – at least it was a secret he had kept from Lerade. It was something that only he and Cal Roney knew. Back in the war, he had turned tail and cracked. In fact, he had been in tears, a man racked by fear, trembling, hiding in an old barn a few miles from the battle which had seared him, burned into his soul, frightened him to the bone. Cal Roney had been the man who had found him in that state, a man on his knees, praying for his life, begging the Good Lord to save him. Deserters would be shot.

Cal Roney had found him and helped him. Through a long, cold night in Missouri he had kept watch over Matt Calero, and somehow dished up some broth, made by the farmer there. They had made it back to the regiment, and nothing was said. The episode was covered over when Cal Roney had wounded him in the arm, to draw some blood and give him a cover story. Struggling back with a bleeding man was a convincing ploy in front of the infantry that Roney had commanded. Even more heartening for the situation was that Calero was a mere private. The men had watched their officer come back, dragging one of their own, having saved his life.

Calero took his time because the truth was, he didn't want to meet Cal in any difficult situation. It would be fine to drink with him, but not to be in a tight spot. Their paths had not crossed since the war apart from one brief meeting in Laramie when Calero had been in a crowd of detectives and Cal had not recognized him.

The plan is, then, he thought as he ambled along, to arrive too late for anything. Whatever it was that ravaged his dreams, he didn't want it back again. Today, four years after the war, Matt Calero still had the bad dreams, the re-run of his shameful fleeing from the noise of the guns and the scream-ing, pain-racked wounded. He still thought of Cal Roney finding him weeping and trembling in that barn. He didn't want reminders of that.

Even out in the open plain, when he made ready to sleep under the stars, comforted by a bottle of whiskey, because he was heading for some place where Cal Roney might be, he knew the bad dreams would torture him, and he drank to try to drop into a deep sleep, where the booze would help him forget.

Cal decided not to follow White Hat. He couldn't move fast enough. Instead, he walked out, pulling Jim Kenny, where he could be seen from the house and called out for Cy and the others. They came out, still gripping their firearms.

'They've gone . . . but they'll be back,' Cal said, 'I winged this one . . . Mr Kenny himself!' He said nothing about what was really in his thoughts: the disturbing discovery of the man in the white hat.

'A Kenny is he, this man . . . the brother of the one who came a few days ago?' Lizzie asked. 'I thought he was a likeable man at first . . . real friendly . . . then it turned out he was nothin' but a threat to us. Well done, Mr Boldwood. He is your brother, mister?' She looked down at Jim, who now sat on the ground.

Sedge advised that they all get back inside and fortify the place. 'Unless, of course, you all want to run.' But Cal could now see the peril in their situation. He had been listening and learning about the Kenny outfit, and he knew they were truly dangerous.

'Cy, maybe you should move on. Do you know who you're dealing with here?'

'Yeah, some crazy brothers who want my home. They can't have it. Now I got one of them!'

'You understate things, my friend,' Cal said. 'This man I just shot is a part of what could be called a private army, ain't that right, son? They'll now want me dead . . . I think they'll be a little upset that we have one of them right here . . . They'll come back and flatten this place. What do you want to do?'

They all looked at each other. There was head-scratching and frowning. Finally, Lizzie said, 'Mr Boldwood, we're not long married. We've seen hard times, Cy and me. When we met up with Sedge here, we found a kindred spirit. . . a man who was badly wounded in the tail end of the war, and who had nobody and nothing. The three of us together became real tired of drifting around, and then, as if guided by the good Lord, we stumbled on this place. Mr Boldwood, we've been runnin' since we was no bigger than a new-born calf. I don't know what Sedge thinks, but I want to stand and fight.'

Sedge agreed. 'Mr Boldwood, I don't know who you are, but this ain't your fight. You were on your way, passin' through, and now you've shot a Kenny here . . . the kid of the family, I reckon. . . . His big brother will be aimin' to bury you alive and dance on the grave. This ain't your fight. No cowardice in swinging your leg over that beautiful appaloosa and steamin' out of this place.'

'My brothers'll rip your guts out, you idiots. Get out of here if you've any sense!' Jim snapped.

Before Cal could answer, Cy butted in with, 'By the way, who exactly are you, Mr Boldwood? I mean, you're handy with a rifle, you took control of the situation in there . . . you're not just a cowherd surely?'

'Some cowherds are useful with weapons, Cy, you know that.'

Cy was about to say something more when there was a sound of hoofs not far off, and their heads turned.

'They can't be here so quick, surely!' Sedge said.

'Back inside, everybody!' Cal called out, and they

115

moved sharp, back into the shack, with Cal picking up his own rifle from his saddle, and giving Bella some fuss. Cy and Sedge grabbed a tight hold of their prisoner and took him inside.

Only a few hundred yards away, Ben Stile, Charlie and Emilia were pulling up to a canter, and they had no idea what had been happening at the Creek.

Riding towards Long Corral at the head of twenty of his cowhands and hired killers, Eddie Kenny knew that the time had come for a show of strength. Jake knew what he was to do, and that would be the last act in the night's drama. First there was the jail-house and its noble but thick-headed deputy, Ben Stile. Here was a man, he thought, riding in the late afternoon light towards the main street, who didn't have the sense to step across the road and join the winners. He was a loser. He was king of the losers. Now he was about to join the feathered choir in the Heaven of the God that he and his suited do-gooders loved so much.

By his side, Jake was feeling his heart throbbing with the thrill of what was coming. His assignment was to kill a man, take a life, put Octavius Gibbs among the corpses in the town cemetery, next to where his good wife lay. He was probably doing good, sending a man to meet his one true love, in the other life that we all have to fall into sometime. Only Gibbs's time was very near. He was not to let his brother down. A

116

voice inside him was urging him on, do the right thing, do a clean job, give the man a quick death.

They arrived at the end of town and Eddie raised a hand to pull them up, so he could savour the moment.

'Right boys, now . . . you three with the dynamite, get down the right-hand side, and it's growing a little dark, so let's have the sticks in place real quick.' The men did as they were told.

'Jake, you wait down the side of the Heath. When we come across, you walk in first and do the job.'

Jake nodded, 'Sure, Eddie. You can rely on me!'

'Now the rest of you, rifles raised. We're gonna charge that jail, as soon as the blast has done its job, and tear it to pieces. We charge when I raise my hand again.'

Jake rode on ahead and turned down a yard out of the distance that the blast would hit. Everyone else stayed where they were and waited. They were far enough away to see the work that the blast would do, but their mounts would be safely away from it, and so would their own heads and ears.

It was a tense few minutes. There was a light in the jail, but nobody in Eddie Kenny's gang waiting there had any notion of who was in the building. In fact, there was only one person in there: a drunk who lay asleep in a cell, on a hard wooden bench, snoring and deeply unaware of what was about to happen.

There was no sound but the jingling and shuffling of riders and saddles along the street, and some music from the Heath, where Macky Heath had welcomed a couple of fiddlers along to entertain. It could have been any normal night in summer when folks walk out and enjoy the entertainment. But Kenny had other plans.

Then there was a mighty blast of noise, and the walls and roof were lifted up into the air for a few seconds, followed by the splintered planks and lats showering the dust. A massive cloud of dust and powdered wood shot into the evening air, and shouts from across the street followed the noise as all the debris hit the ground and spread outwards. After a strange peace of a few seconds, people ran out of buildings towards the wrecked jail, and some shouted 'Take care . . . stand back . . . there may be more blasts!'

That was the sign for Eddie Kenny and his boys to charge forwards and start shooting at any pieces of wall that still remained upright. They made such a thorough job of this that even the iron bars in their frames clattered down to the ground. The people who had started to run out now turned back, screaming in fear.

Folk in Long Corral would talk about that night for years to come. They would recall the blast, and the appearance of the great intimidating gang of Kenny's men – but they would all tell the tale of what happened in the Heath Hotel.

It should have been a simple enough task. A man was to be shot dead. But earlier that night, when the Heath brothers, Sonny Gibbs and the other members of the former *Informer* paper normally gathered for their poker, they were missing. Jake Kenny found this out when he walked in, shoved aside a man who stood in his way, swaying with the effects of drink, and walked up to the card table in the back room, ready to draw his revolver and put a bullet in Gibbs' forehead. Jake saw, in that instant, that there was no Sonny Gibbs. In fact, there was no one except a servant who was cleaning the table top.

Jake did not draw his gun. The servant told him that the men had gone out to see what the explosion was. Common sense told Jake to skulk away somewhere and return later.

'You wanted to join in the game, Mister Kenny?' the man asked.

'Sure, sure. I'll come back when they're settled again.'

Jake found a quiet room where a few old men were reading or chatting, mostly about the explosion. Someone rushed in and told them that the jailhouse had been blown up, and they muttered and mumbled their surprise, but went on enjoying the peace and quiet. A few nodded at Jake, who sat and melted into the background, waiting for the gamblers to return.

People kept shouting at the door that the jail was blown to pieces. But after a while one of the news-mongers told the old men that Ben Stile had not been in the building, and that he had set off for Blood Creek.

Jake would bide his time, let the furore die down, and when the card players were back, he would strike.

Out at Blood Creek, the newest arrivals had ridden up to the front of the shack and Cy had recognized them, so that when Ben called out to see if all was well, Cy went out to the porch and invited them all inside.

In seconds, as they gathered in the lamp light, Ben Stile's inspection of the place found Cal. 'So, Cal Roney . . . we meet again. Under that beard I can now see the eyes and the shape of your face and build! It's him all right, Emilia. Cal Roney, it seems I owe you my life – twice over. I'd like to shake your hand and forget about the past, though Gibbs is of another mind. He doesn't know you're here, yet.'

They shook hands. 'Ben, your sister is the best nurse this side of the Mississippi!' Cal said, putting an arm around Emilia. He couldn't avoid noticing the look he got from Charlie, who was now intro-duced to him.

'This is all very cheery and friendly,' Sedge said, 'But there's a small army on its way to destroy us and flatten this place to the ground. Reckon we ought to do somethin' afore we're pushin' up flowers in the churchyard, folks!'

Charlie was now whispering something to Emilia, and Cy was reassuring Lizzie that all was well; Ben looked around the room, his mind thinking of defending the place, and Sedge was preparing bread and cold meat for all. A natural leader would have seen what was to be done, and that was Cal. In one corner, on the floor, was Jim Kenny, tied hands and feet, looking restless. Emilia had found an old shirt, torn some cloth from it and bound Jim's wounded arm. The bullet had splintered the edge of a bone and gone through him.

Cal instinctively stood at the end of the table, and had them all sitting down. 'Look,' he said, studying the faces of everyone there, 'I was just passing through here. I should have moved on by now, but I can't leave you here to face your Kenny brood, kid . . . big brother's not too happy, I expect?'

'You bet, mister. Eddie and Jake will slice you in two for this. I'd run if I was you, folks. You should let me go now and run for it while you have the chance.'

'Ignore the man,' Cal said, 'Now look, this is gonna be a siege. Unless you want to ride back to town now, and chance meeting the gang there. Chances are that would happen and you would be caught in the open, and circled, then cut down, real easy. Now, I been an officer for the Union, and with your permission I'll lead our defence. It's a siege and we have the advantage. Believe me ... out-numbered or not.'

Sedge said, 'I knew you was ... I could tell. Where was you, mister?'

'I was in most places with Sherman ... my night-mares mostly concern the siege at Atlanta, and if I learned anything about standing with your tails up, it was there, as I faced the men who were doing just that.'

Sedge dished out the food and for a few minutes they ate in silence, listening to Cal. Jim was given food as well, and took it like a ravenous hound, with no thanks.

'We treat this as the first position to hold,' Cal said, 'But make ready another position behind to fall back into, and then a third. We keep moving back, and gradually Kenny's men thin out, so in the end, we'll have a real advantage ... Cary Island. I see out there beyond the lean-to, Sedge, you have some old tables and chairs. That's our barricade. We make that now, as soon as we've eaten. That's where we fall back, because as sure as I know my horse likes sugar, Kenny's gonna burn this shack. Maybe even blast it.'

'He'll surround the place and come at you from all sides, mister!' Jim said, with the tone of a tor-menter relishing seeing suffering in his victims.

'Jim, you can answer a question for me. . . .' Cal walked across to him. 'The man in the white hat with the limp, who is he?'

'Why that's Coop, Wichita Cooper. His Bowie knife is waiting for your gizzard.'

'Cooper? He's mine, everybody. He's mine. You hear?' Cal looked around. They nodded and agreed.

The next hour was a busy one. While Lizzie stood with a rifle pointed at Jim's head, the others made the circle of furniture and old crates about a hundred yards from the back of the shack, at the edge of the creek. Cal checked all this and was happy with it. He then pointed out to Cary Island and said, 'That's the third position.'

'Was you a good officer, Mr Boldwood?' Sedge asked. 'You sure seem a useful man to have around.'

'I used my common sense, Mr Gulley. Now everybody, understand this . . . the aim is for us all to be safely at Cary's Island. . . it'll be dark. We'll move under moonlight. But from there, we have the advantage. They'll have to come through the water, and we'll be under good cover!'

When all the preparations were done, they all sat down around the table again. Cal had brought Bella into better cover at the far side of the old rotting barn to the north; Sedge killed any hint of a flame or heat in his cooking lean-to, and all weapons were checked. All lamps were extinguished then, and it

123

was quiet – apart from the commentary from Jim Kenny, still on the floor in the corner.

'Now this is all a waste of your precious time, folks . . . don't listen to this madman! Whatever you do, you face forty or fifty men! This here military man . . . he's loco, I tell you. Stay here and die. I'll enjoy watching you, folks!'

Cy crawled across to the prisoner and stuffed a bandanna into his mouth, raising a laugh and improving the morale of the little group.

'Now,' said Ben Stile, 'As I am the lawman around here, I have to say that my worry is for you ladies . . . we're in a tight corner here, and we might not get out.'

'I'm staying with you, Ben,' Emilia said. Then came just a little observation, but it shattered Cal's thoughts about the woman and what he had been considering saying to her. Charlie was sitting by her, and Emilia put out her hand and gently touched his. They looked at each other, and anyone could see that they cared, and that their feelings were sincere.

Cal's ruminations on what he felt about her and how she was the woman he had dreamed about, were crushed. He had nobody to tell about it, but since riding out of Long Corral, he had been unable to resist thoughts of her and how, after all his wandering years, she would be the perfect woman to settle down with, raise a family, stop drifting and do something else instead of chasing rogues and bandits across the plains and up the valleys. The thought of making justice happen was important to him, but maybe meeting Emilia was fate telling him that he had done more than his share of lawman work and that it was time to rest up.

His thoughts were interrupted by a noise outside, and he darted to the window. Something or someone had moved across the undergrowth, and all the men were looking intently outside; then someone said, 'Some kind o' critter! Rest easy!' It was Sedge, who had the best eyesight of them all, and also a sixth sense, which was why he always said he was still alive, as far as he could tell.

Now only a few miles from Long Corral, Matt Calero heard the explosion and saw the smoke. He knew he should have dug in his spurs and raced to the scene. There was most likely some trouble and he was a Pinkerton man: he should be there. But it seemed probable that Cal Roney was not there, where the noise was, as his mission was to be at Blood Creek. He decided to ride around and miss out the town. Deep inside, he sensed that trouble was stirring, and like it or not, he would have to intervene. He would have to force himself to ride in and fight with, or fight for, Cal Roney. He owed him something, sure he did. He owed him a lot. But his conscience was nagging at him, telling him to take the easy way out, and that voice was fighting with the knowledge that he had to do the right thing.

NINE

In Long Corral, Eddie and his men were inspecting the ruins of the jail, and a crowd had gathered; they were staring into the ruins and asking questions. There was smoke and dust everywhere, and the Kenny hands were stalking around, coughing and complaining. It had been a case of overkill. They had managed to shatter a wall of another building next door, part of a leather store. Dirt was blasted at passers-by a hundred yards up the road.

'Damn me, you men . . . that corpse ain't Deputy Stile . . . it's that no-good drunk that curses the world and should now be glad to be free of it . . . we did him a favour! But where's Stile?'

His men shook their heads. One said, 'He's sure hard to kill, that man, considerin' he has no friends and walks alone, he's no right to be still breathin', boss!'

'Yeah. Now we can only hope he's over the road

playin' cards and so Jake's like to take him out of the picture along with Gibbs. We'll wait for the sound of a shot and then get over there.'

But his men were out asking around to find where the lawman was, and they were told that he was seen riding out towards Blood Creek. Eddie commented that if he went out there he would only find bodies, as long as Jim and Coop had done the job.

In the Heath Hotel, the card players were assembling again to play, and the musicians were back in their seats. The townsfolk had found out that deputy Stile had not been in the place, and Sonny Gibbs had noted that whoever had done it had done them a favour. It was only when someone ran in to say that Eddie Kenny and his men had blasted the place that he sat up, with the others, and wondered what should be done.

'Well, if he's here with his men, then he means business,' Macky Heath said.

'Sure . . . maybe this place is next!' His brother added.

'No,' Gibbs said. 'Think about it, he has nothing to gain by flattening the Heath. The jail, yes, he maybe thought that Ben was inside, but he won't touch this place – he wants to run it.'

Then into the card room came Jake Kenny. He was flushed, excited, and he betrayed bad nerves in every little movement he made. The older men, severe and serious in their evening dress, looked him up and down. 'You want something, son?' Gibbs asked.

Jake pulled out his pistol and stood with the barrel pointed at Gibbs. His hand was shaking and his voice trembled. 'Mr Gibbs . . . you printed that paper . . . you told damned lies about us . . . your time has come!'

The Heaths and their friends ducked, raising their hands, and all mumbled, 'Easy now son. . . !' But Gibbs never moved an inch, and he faced the barrel with equanimity, and his courageous stare unnerved Jake Kenny. This gave Gibbs just time enough to lunge forwards and make a grab for Jake's leg. He had been told that, when faced with a gun, the best move was to dive forwards and head for the shooter's feet, not to turn away and widen the scope for the shot. This was good advice, as Jake fired low and by the time he did, Gibbs had a hold of the younger man's legs and wrestled him to the floor. The bullet ripped into the floorboards.

The other men stood back as another shot was fired, this time into the ceiling, as Gibbs forced Jake on to his back and managed to punch him on the cheek. The gun fell to the floor, and Gibbs swung another blow at Jake's face. This time he went out like a light. But a voice at the door said, 'Oh dear, you just attacked my little brother. Shame. You have to die for that.'

This was Eddie, who had come across with his men. He had Coop at his side, and Coop had all the information Eddie needed about the Creek and who was there.

But Gibbs was not going to die that night. No sooner had he heard the words spoken than he snatched the gun from the floor and pointed it at Eddie before he could draw.

'I wouldn't do that, Mister Gibbs. . . there's no law in town, seeing as how Ben Stile has ridden out to Blood Creek. Stile is there, along with Cal Roney – back from the dead, I reckoned, when I saw him! We're going out there to send them to Hell!' Coop said this with a tone of cruelty.

But he didn't finish the sentence. Gibbs, pointing the pistol at him, had the drop on Eddie and his men, and he backed out, facing them until he reached the door, then he ran for the first horse in the stables.

Out at the Creek, the waiting went on. It was a situation in which a man felt cornered, backed up in darkness and waiting for anything or nothing. It made fear, generated it so that in the mind, it was like waiting for a dam to burst or for lightning to strike. Cal, remembering the desperate confrontations in the war, walked slowly around, treating the men and women as his military company. They all had rifles and side-arms, and he had packed just the one room, with the lean-to open behind. There was a clear way through. The wait gave him time to think, and he knew that the one weakness was if Kenny's men circled the place as soon as they arrived. He decided to tell Ben Stile this, and made it clear what was the only course of action.

There was a hostage, of course. They had Jim Kenny, but he was wounded, and would slow them down when they moved. Locking him up was the safest bet, and Cy and Ben were assigned to gag him and shut him in the one place which had potential as a jail – Sedge's pantry. He was hog-tied and couldn't make a sound.

'Ben, I'll have to go and sit in place outside, just the other side of the circle of furniture, right? From there I'll see any movement if they surround the place. . . and I'm sure they will. I'll pick off anyone who slithers around there.'

'Be careful Cal . . . and by the way, let's forget what happened to Mrs Gibbs . . . in my book, you're redeemed, my friend.'

'I hope the other folk think the same,' Cal said, and crouching low, headed off into the dark beyond the old barn.

'You were supposed to have a reason to hand over this place to me,' Eddie Kenny said to the Heath brothers. They were still in that back room, and Jake had made a mess of things again. Eddie's patience was frayed, and he laid it on the line to the Heaths now.

'Tomorrow, Mr Holden is going to bring a bill of sale here, a bill accepting that I have paid you five hundred dollars for this place . . . You will sign this and give it to Mr Holden. If you refuse to sign, then you will both be shot dead by sundown, wherever you are. I been a patient man far too long. Now, if you think I'm being too extreme and unreasonable about this, then you have the option of leaving town. If you get lost and keep ridin' till you reach the sea or the northern wilderness, you might survive, but to be honest, if you stay here and sign, I'll keep you on as bar staff. Deal?' He held out his hand and put on the kind of smile that would annoy even a drunk preacher, it looked so falsely pleasant.

The Heath brothers looked at each other. For so long they had sat tight and refused to co-operate with Kenny. Now he had lost patience and was doing things the old-fashioned way, how they did things before anyone wore a tin star or called himself a mayor.

Doc Heath was the first to react. He held out a hand, and Kenny shook it. Macky followed. But to Eddie's mind, it had all been too easy – suspiciously easy. He gave them a sideways stare and frowned. 'Pleasure doin' business with you, my friends. You'll not regret this.'

Macky knew, from long experience, that his

brother was not serious in what they had done, and that there was a plan in his head. He played along, and when Doc invited Eddie to play a hand, it was irresistible.

'But we have to get out to Blood Creek, boss!' Coop complained.

'You men go. I'll follow, when I've won this game.'

Eddie and the Heath brothers settled in for a game. 'I got a neat notion to put to you, Eddie Kenny,' Macky said. 'How about we play for real money . . . say a thousand bucks first?'

'We could, only I can't lose you see, because I don't obey no rules. If you win, I'll just take the money back, with a gun barrel stuck on your jaw.' Eddie smiled.

'Fine . . . just a little bit of pleasantry, Mister Kenny. We are gentlemen after all, and if you do assume ownership of the Heath, I'd like to think you will maintain its dignified and cultured nature.' Macky put on the front he had always used in his rise, as a gambler on the river, when he was raising funds to buy a place of his own. It impressed Kenny.

'You know, Heath, you'd better sign that bill, as I need a man like you to run the place . . . a man of culture, of refinement. Now tell your man here to deal.'

It took some time for Macky to win the imagined amount of cash they were pretending to play for. He

133

couldn't resist taunting Eddie a little as he won each hand. And every time he teased and ribbed his opponent, Macky took another glass of whiskey, and in spite of his brother's whispered advice to slow down, he kept on, and Eddie followed suit. After half an hour, they were both the worse for drink, and Doc was sensing the beginnings of an idea at the back of his mind. It was a mistake. He saw that only a few men had stayed behind after Coop and Jake had left for the Creek, and he looked at Eddie's pistol in the holster, so close that it could easily be snatched. As Eddie's words slurred and he swayed in his seat, his men behind urged him to pack it in and get out of town.

'Ah, Coop and Jake will have taken the place by now. You boys be patient, huh?'

He delayed, and took even more drink. When Doc Heath saw the Kenny men relax and walk out into the main bar, he seized his chance and took the gun. But Eddie shouted, and it was loud, so loud that Doc soon saw his mistake. His mind was set on using Eddie as a hostage, but Eddie's men were quick: before Doc could take hold of him, half-a-dozen of his men were firing at him and at Macky from the door, and Eddie rolled on to the floor, coming to rest under a long side-table. One of the bullets hit him in the leg.

In the volley of bullets that were shot into the room, Macky was hit in the face and chest and he fell back, dead. The dealer crawled to the floor and begged for mercy as the men advanced towards them, and Doc screamed his brother's name and shuffled across to him, some shots still coming his way. But though he had lost his brother, he was saved, as Eddie, behind, shrieked out that he needed the doc.

'Don't hurt Doc Heath . . . I'm hit, I'm hit, boys!'

The shooting stopped and the Kenny boys lifted their boss on to the side table, where there was enough room for the doc to look at him. But Doc was crouching over his brother, cursing Eddie Kenny. 'He's dead . . . he's dead, you murdering bastards . . . this is all you know, killing! You can rot, Kenny . . . I'm doing nothing!'

Eddie Kenny had a problem. He had a major bleed as the bullet had hit an artery and his life blood was spurting out like a fall over a mountain course. He yelled for a tourniquet and one of the men grabbed a cloth from off the table and wrapped it around the leg.

'Looks like your fibular artery, Eddie . . . you could lose a lot of blood.'

'You heartless swine . . . get over here or die!' Eddie snapped, taking his Colt and cocking it, then pointing the barrel at Doc, with his hand trembling.

'Looks like you have a shattered *lateral malleolus*, my friend!' Doc said, enjoying the tormenting of this man whom he rated lower than a rat.

'You shoot him and you're dead, Eddie!' One of the men shouted.

'Looks like you're in a parlous state, Mr Kenny. You know, you need a physician!'

Doc started to laugh, though he was hurting real bad under that front. He was still keeping one arm wrapped around his brother, whom he had confirmed in his mind was dead.

Eddie's mind was in a whirl. The cloth was soaked with blood. He started to feel faint. 'I thought you medical men took some kind of oath. . . .'

'Ah, that's only to save the lives of folks who are of some use to humanity. In your case, you're no more than a lice crawling in a corpse's eyeball.'

The Kenny men all screamed and shouted for Doc to do something, but he played his game a little longer. Then, knowing that Eddie would be close to passing out, he went for his bag in the next room, telling the Kenny boys what he was doing.

When he came back, he bawled out orders for clean water. Eddie was now shouting out with pain and with the thought that he was bleeding to death. Doc Heath had had to push the fact that his brother was dead deep down inside him. He couldn't let a man die, even the man who had taken his brother's life. He called out more orders to the men standing by, and gathered all the materials he needed. 'Kenny, you're going to pass out . . . get a big pull of this brandy down you. It's likely to hurt more than you can imagine. If I don't stitch up this cut, you'll die in a matter of minutes!' He started sewing up the cut, leaving the bullet damage alone until that was done. The slug had gone through, slicing tissue and muscle. Eddie Kenny was out cold now.

Out at the Creek, Jake and their men were moving into position around the shack. They could see gun-barrels at the windows. 'I count five,' Coop said. 'Who do we know is in there?'

'We don't,' Jake said, puzzled.

'Well, seems there's five. We got thirty men.'

Jake looked to Coop, as the experienced man, for leadership. 'You were with Pa . . . you seen every-thing, Coop. What's best? We burn the place down?'

Coop looked around and thought for a minute. 'No point in overkill. Anyway, there are some ques-tions to answer, and corpses can't talk. I mean, what's the man Roney doing here? He's a useful man in a scrap, and I heard he went into the war. He's learned somethin' there, son. What we do is just fire for cover while two or three men run in to squat by the doors. We get some men around the back as well. Jake, pick the best two hand-fighters to go around the back and watch any door.'

The men crouched and ran, crouched and ran, in turn, until they were in position by the lean-to, behind the nearest scrub. Cal's plan worked out fine: he could see them both very clearly, and they had no notion he was there.

Coop picked out three men to run in, and lined up all the others except a man left with the horses. Then he tested the defenders, and ordered: 'After a count of three, fire at the windows!' When this happened, in a second, a rattle of shots cut a line across the side of the shack, and it was so fierce that planks were loosened and shattered. From inside, Sedge ordered to fire back, to the location of the shots. There were no casualties.

What this did was alert Octavius Gibbs, who was now close to the Creek, and when he heard the gunfire he dismounted and shinned up a rock to where he could see something of what was happening. Under the moonlight, he could see Coop's white hat and three or four men moving around near him. He saw the shack and barn, and he could make out the barrels at the window. He had gone out there searching for Cal Roney, thinking it could be man to man, and he had stumbled on a battle.

He had never been so confused. All he knew was that probably in that building there was the man whose bullet had killed the young wife he had loved. Other than that, there was someone else in there, and an army of the Kenny brothers. He was there, and he was armed, but there was only one person he felt any malice about, and he was in the midst of all this crazy shooting. But if he had to take sides, he thought, it would be to help the folks inside see off the attackers.

In his hide-out, Cal could see everything that was going on to the rear, and he had only the two men to take care of. There was nothing for it but to cut them down and then wait for Ben Stile to lead the retreat out through the lean-to. They were sitting down behind a thick fallen log, just the right height to rest a rifle on, and they were watching the back door. From where Cal was, he could see the two heads and shoulders. He didn't like killing, but it was them or him, and he was sure that the man with the white hat was capable of any iniquity and would have no restraint if he was let loose on the women in that shack, and young Charlie wasn't exactly a seasoned fighter, so the odds were stacked against the defenders. Two less would help.

He took aim at the first man. What was needed was a clean shot through the back of the head, and fortunately the man was still, sighting his own target, no doubt concentrating on the door through which folk would run. Cal's aim was true and steady: the trigger squeezed and the bullet sent home, bursting into the soft flesh at the base of the man's head, between the two muscles at the back. He lurched forwards with a yell, and in a split second, his partner turned to look up. There was just the right moment presented then: a face to put a second bullet home, into the head right above the nose. He fell, quick and definite. Neither man moved again.

Cal ran down to check on them, and then took their position, when he was sure that they were gone. There was no chance of them clouding a mirror, and that gave him peace of mind. The question now was, how soon would the others come through that door? Inside, the second enfilade of rifle fire had wrecked a line of wood and dislodged a window frame. It was risky for anyone to fire back. Ben had darted quick as a jack-rabbit into a space and fired where he saw smoke, but everything was defensive, and there had been some close shaves, with bullets tearing into walls just inches from Emilia's head, and one shot slamming into a vase which Lizzie had brought with her from home and treasured.

'Let's git out the back . . . Cal's waitin' for us . . .' Ben shouted, and he let them go first, while he moved with his back to them, looking towards the window and door in case the Kenny boys were on the move and ready to smash their way in. He was right. One man came through the door after kicking it in, and Ben hit him in the chest with his first shot.

'Come on folks . . . real snappy now!' he screamed out. In a few seconds they were aware of Cal shouting out for them to come to him. One by one they reached the log and leapt over it, lining up by Cal. Finally, Ben Stile came out, and ran straight for cover by the log.

'We have to move back directly to Cary Island!' Cal called, and he had them moving back in a line, seeing some of Kenny's men now emerge from the lean-to. They saw their prey retreating, and Cal, covering the retreat, saw Jake and the white hat come out behind their men. He decided that he had time for one last shot before he followed the others to the Creek. He stepped back and shot from the hip. The shot brought down another man, though it was meant for the white hat, whom he had now marked as his own. Before he left that place, he swore to himself, he would bring down the man who had killed his father.

At the edge of the Creek, the others were wading across to the little island. The water was waist high most of the way, but there was a deeper channel around twenty feet from the island shore, and the women were swimming this now, with the men close behind.

Cal was sure that the Kenny men would be moving quickly and might be able to fire from the shore as the party of defenders fought their way across.

He was right, and he was the last into the Creek. As he reached the deeper part, where he knew he would have to swim, he held his gun high; he heard

141

shouts from behind. He could make out Jake's cry 'Shoot now boys . . . they're in range!'

Jake had found his little brother Jim by then, and seeing Jim wounded riled him even more. It was a mistake. He stopped thinking clearly and had to put up with the ranting and red-faced rage of Jim, who kept on snapping out the same word, that he wanted them all dead, all dead, for what they had done to him. He had to be content with a back seat as the action developed, sitting in the stables, seething with anger.

Bullets came to Cal's side, missing him narrowly. But Cal couldn't fight, he couldn't turn, and the chances were he would be hit. He shouted for someone to give him covering fire, and he saw the blurred outline of Sedge through the water as he swam. Sedge knelt on the muddy edge of the island and fired some shots across. Then there was a loud, deafening sound of rifle fire, seeming like a whole company of men had sent a volley into the enemy. There was a cry of pain and someone on the island shouted, 'Sedge. . . they got Sedge!' It was a woman's voice.

It was considerably later and darker now, and near the island there were boughs and dead trees reaching into the water, so Cal made for the nearest and gripped a thick bough, fighting to get his breath back.

He didn't know it, but fifty yards away, Lizzie was

weeping over the dead body of her friend Sedge Gulley, and Cy was screeching in panic for her to leave him and come back to cover.

TEN

Dug in now on Cary island, Ben, Cy and Cal had the others out of sight, while they stood watch, squatting higher up, above two large rocks which formed the main little fortress that Cary the recluse had made for himself. It was a perfect hole to bolt into if you were in trouble. The strange old character had done well all those years back. Everybody still had their rifles clasped close, and Ben had thought to bring ammunition. There was tension in the air, so tight you could feel it pressing on the skin.

Charlie, sitting with the women, hunched at the back of the earthy hollow that Cary had dug out of the rock side, saw how cut up Lizzie was about her friend, and he did his best to comfort her. But there was no time for sentiment, as they all knew. There were plenty of men on the far side of that Creek who would be able to get across. But there was a great advantage in being above the water level, and being able to see every movement over at the homestead.

Cal, Ben and Cy knew this as well, lying flat and watching the night, praying that dawn would come soon. 'Our best chance is to bide our time ... let them decide how much they want to risk an open attack,' Cal said. 'Question is, does Eddie Kenny want this place bad enough to risk so many men?'

'I know the man,' Ben put in. 'When he wants somethin' done, he'll stop at nothin'. He fixes on what he hates and does everythin' to destroy it, regardless of what he might lose.'

'My kind of madman,' Cal smiled. As he said this, he was thinking of white hat, and he wanted to know more about him. Ben Stile knew. 'Now Cal, the white hat is Coop. He's Wichita Cooper. So many times I've tried to have him shut away, but he always escaped ... Kenny protected him. He's Eddie's number two. The boys will let him lead.'

'They're not likely to starve us out ... not enough patience for that,' Cal said, 'So I reckon somethin' bold will win the day.' This was the time that Cy had been waiting for, and his feelings poured out.

'Look, Mr Roney ... Mr Stile, I haven't your experience in these matters. My only thought is for Lizzie ... and the other woman, Emilia, too. I

145

mean, I'm a married man. I have to put my woman first. We was doin' fine here, making it a home, if you understand? I know you two men are loners. You see the world different to me. I was here with my best friend and my new wife, hoping that the world might leave us alone a while. It did, and we had some time to build relationships, to let habits set in. But I always knew that the badness would come in, like a wound, on a good, healthy body. Fact is, I couldn't bear to lose my Lizzie . . . I already lost my best partner out there. Me and Sedge been through a whole mess o' trouble, and we seen the best of each other. I'm gonna miss him like I lost a limb.'

This was not the tough, heartless robber that the Pinkertons had in their files, Cal thought. He was starting to feel that destiny had decided that on this mission, he might be able to get his man – but would he want to? Duty was pulling at him from one side, and sentiment from another.

'*Cal Roney*,' he said to himself, laying there with his eyes fixed on the shore, '*you always wanted to fight for justice, protect the weak against the strong without scruples. Now see you today . . .*'

Then something inside gave him an idea. It was crazy, but the thought was there. Now things had changed: the hunt for Cy Felder had been eclipsed by the need to send Coop to the next world for what he had done. Maybe white hat would fight him for the victory, in a duel, like in the battles of the old days. He started raising the topic to Ben, when a shower of bullets came at them, tearing into rock and earth on both sides. 'Fire at the smoke!' Ben called out.

There was enough light now for targets to be seen. Coop and Jake's men knew that they were more vulnerable, and they would be the ones who would have to move.

For what seemed to the defenders like half an hour but was only a few minutes, both sides fired wildly and rapidly at each other. Then there was a pause. 'Sixteen shots . . . they all got Henry rifles!' Ben said, 'Same as us, apart from Lizzie's old thing. This could go on all day!'

Cal took his chance now, but as he spoke, a voice called from over the Creek, cutting off his suggestion of a duel. 'Listen up you folks . . . this is Jake Kenny. We don't want no blood-bath today. No, we're here for just one person – the deputy Ben Stile. He owes us. Would we want this old wreck of a place? Think about it. No, Ben Stile, you walk out over here and we'll leave with you.'

Cy was the first to speak. 'He's as double-minded as a fox. I tell you, after what we did to his brother, he wants us all out of his life for good.

'Yeah, Kenny wants this place as a base to work against the new homesteaders . . . he wants the territory between here and Laramie, and beyond to the main rivers. It's them or us today.'

Cal dismissed his notion of a duel. It was no guarantee of any solution. But Ben saw a white flag go up into sight and Jake spoke again. 'Now Ben, let you and me talk. White flag. . . .'

Ben stood up and crept to the end of the rock, then rested on his bent legs, keeping his gun handy.

Jake Kenny had his marksman in place, ready to shoot at Ben. 'The fool believes me,' he said, 'Pick him off, cowboy!' The man aimed his barrel at Ben and was ready to press the trigger – but he was hit from behind, and with a moan of pain, rolled down off his place on a thick log, to lie dead in the dust. His shot went wide of the mark, and Ben ducked down again. In the line of men sitting with Jake, all heads turned to see who was shooting from behind them. They couldn't see Gibbs, who had decided that standing against Kenny was more satisfying than hunting for Roney.

It was Gibbs' turn to play false now, and he put in a full round of bullets, strafing the line of men with Kenny. They had prepared nothing for an attack from behind, and they were easy prey. Several men fell, and Jake and Coop ran for cover to the lean-to. They were thinking that a dozen men now lay behind them and that they were trapped.

From where they were, Cal and the other men could not see all this, but they heard the shots and they saw men fall.

'Thank the good Lord,' called Ben, 'Help has arrived . . . maybe the sheriff is back after all, and we've heard only lies about him!'

There would never be a better opportunity to get even, Cal was thinking. It was a moment to be seized, as there was now panic among the Kenny men, who were inside the shack, and reduced in numbers. The tide had turned. Cal told everyone to follow him after five minutes had passed, and to wait for his call. He ran across the water, paddling, swimming, then walking, his gunbelt and pistols held high, and he shouted for Coop. As soon as he reached the yard by the lean-to, he shouted, 'Wichita Cooper. . . come out. It's justice time! Me and you . . . nobody else.'

There was a silence which seemed to last ages. Then a voice called from the shack, 'Who's talking?'

'Do you recall a time when you attacked the Red Saddle?'

A door opened and out walked Coop, into the dry earth, standing with his hands held out, above his guns. 'Red Saddle?'

Cal took a few more steps into the light, out of the shade of the cottonwoods.

'Little homestead, south of the Laramie Mountains. . .you and your roughnecks arrived one day and indulged in some slaughter . . . not for any reason, as far as I could tell. I saw it all. You had a real daunting knife then . . . a Bowie. I saw it all.'

149

'Can't recall, mister. Who are you?'

'You took the life of a man called Roney and his wife . . . the worst killers in the *Comancheria* would not have done what you did that day, and I seen them kill, too.'

Coop's face now showed beads of hot sweat running down it, in runnels to his chin. He wiped his brow with his jacket cuff. 'I ask again, who are you?'

'Name's Roney. Your turn to die, Wichita. Know any prayers? But then, God has no place for you . . . better ask Satan for help, as you're in his outfit.'

'You're Cal Roney? You saw me. . . ?'

'Not so good for a little boy to see what you did. No children watching now, though.'

Coop fixed his stare on Cal, who now thought about calling the others over, but thought better of it. There was too much risk. In the hide-out, the women and Charlie scuttled out to join Ben and Cy. They all tentatively walked into the water, weapons held high, and saw in the distance two dark figures offset by the dry, pale dust.

'No more talking, Coop. Think you're faster than me? Wanna chance it?'

Coop's hand darted down at once, each hand snatching the revolvers by grip and trigger. But he wasn't quick enough: Cal had his Remingtons out in the hot air in less time than it took a lizard to shake its tail, and two bullets lodged in Coop, one through an eye and the other into his heart, which had been beating so fast for the previous minutes that he thought it would burst out through his ribs.

Wichita Cooper died fast. Cal stood over him and said to himself, 'Pa, one shot for you, and Ma, the second for you . . . justice!'

There was a line of men and women behind Cal now, all pointing their weapons at Jake Kenny, whose men were slowly gathering behind him, guns drawn ready. Before anyone could speak, a voice rang out from the stables, and then Octavius Gibbs stepped out, holding his rifle forward, the barrel pointing at Cal. He walked briskly towards him, and when he was close enough for all to hear, he said, 'Ladies and gentlemen, I see that a vendetta has been paid. I, too, came out here to settle a score. I came out to send you, Cal Roney, to the world of shades, but now . . . well. . . .' He threw the rifle down on to the earth. 'I think it's time all this stopped.'

Jake Kenny looked around, wondering what to do and what to say. He wasn't used to making decisions, and now Coop was gone, everything seemed to be pointless. Killing had gone on and on, and for what? He told his men to put away their guns and sat down on the edge of the porch.

'Sometimes a man has to quit, and this is one of them times!'

But nobody saw Jim Kenny. He had finally stirred,

and walked unsteadily towards the sound of the shots, picking up a rifle from a dead man as he went. He came close just as matters were being explained, and there was more talking and reasoning than fighting.

It was Cal's turn to give them one last surprise. He turned around and looked at Cy and Lizzie, now holding hands. He took a pocket-book from his vest and said, 'This here says that Cal Roney is employed by the Pinkerton Detective Agency. . . .'

Cy Felder drew his gun and backed away, nervous.

'Yes, I'm a detective, and I came here looking for Cy Felder. Cy, put the gun away. I never saw you. When I reached Blood Creek, you were long gone!' Cy ran to him and shook his hand.

Cal hadn't finished. He now went to Gibbs. He said, 'If we're talking justice, mister, I thank you. I need to tell you that every day since that awful accident, I've thought about your good wife. I've had nightmares about that day. If you're leaving that debt unpaid then I salute you, as you're a gentleman and a Christian. Will you shake my hand?'

Gibbs did just that.

'Well, if there's any more making up and fancy speeches, I'm heading back to home.' Ben said.

'Unfortunately, you don't have one!' This was Jake, who realized that nobody there knew about the wrecking of the jailhouse. 'It was blowed up real efficiently by my big brother . . . awful sorry, Stile. Casualty of war, I guess. You'll have a new one. A war that I declare over!'

There was an uneasy quiet for a while, but then out from the shade came Jim Kenny. He had been keeping away from all the noise, as his wound was throbbing and giving him constant pain. Now he was just plain mad at the whole world, and wanted to kick anything within range and destroy anyone who attracted his hatred. As he came out, stamping and steaming, his brother met him and explained why there was no more shooting – but Jim pushed him away and lifted his rifle at Cal.

Jim Kenny looked around, seeing the body of Coop, and then some other dead men from the Double T. 'We lost then, brother?'

'No . . . nobody lost and nobody won, Jim.'

'Sure . . . because this man is still alive. Sorry, but I still believe in a vendetta . . . it's good for the soul. This man shot me, could have killed me! Time for him to pay.' He raised his barrel. Cal was about to dive for the man's feet, to close down the angle of range for the shot – but before Jim could fire, there was a crack, and a spot of blood appeared on his throat. He fell like a sapling, hitting the ground hard and fast.

Heads turned as a rider cantered in and slipped down from his horse. He looked at Cal Roney, and

Cal looked back. For a long second or two they showed no emotion on their faces, and then Matt Calero said, 'That's a debt paid, brother!'

ELEVEN

There was something different in the air around Long Corral a few days after the fight at Blood Creek. It was a town that, young as it was, had known the extremes of violence, and that had worn down the sensibilities of its inhabitants. There was a palpable desire for peace, a hunger for a ceasefire, a truce at the least. There were dead and there were wounded, and as always happens in a war, the wounds left with the living were not always on the body. Grief played its part in making that different, most welcome, feeling around the streets. The general opinion was that they were fortunate just to lose one building, and the jokers commented on the fact that there was no place to lock up criminals. But on the whole it was weariness that led to the new, liberating feeling in the town.

Talk around the stores and bars put this down to Eddie Kenny, who was still in bed at Doc Heath's little back-room surgery, where Emilia was caring for him. In the hour after breakfast on the day after the shootings, Eddie had welcomed his brother Jake to the room, and they were talking about what had happened, when Ben Stile arrived. He walked right in and pulled out his pistol.

'Eddie Kenny, Jake Kenny, I'm arresting you for murder. Eddie, you will stay here under surveillance until you're well enough to move, and then I'll be escortin' you to Laramie.' Then he added with a sneer, and not without a touch of humour: 'They have a jail there!'

Eddie had a lot to get off his chest, but neither he nor Jake tried to argue with the law.

'Ben, I know it won't do no good, but I think some mistakes were made over the last week, and bein' so close to my own demise, well, it sure changed an attitude, I guess. I regret the death of Macky and my boys from the Double T of course. . . and the old-timer. Things got out of hand. It was all supposed to work out real smooth.'

'Real smooth with myself and my friends either dead as last year, or workin' for your sick enterprise!' Ben said, trying to hold back the anger he felt. 'Fact is, Kenny, although you're sittin' there leaking blood, I don't believe there's an ounce of remorse in your bones. Now, I'm puttin' away my gun, as I know you were both disarmed, but I have to tell you that I'm not alone now, in my work. . .Come in you two!' He called out, and in came Cal and Matt.

Jake responded with a sigh and a groan. 'Oh hell, you two! Damned Pinkertons, brother . . . the two I told you about.'

Cal looked across to the corner, where Emilia was standing back, keeping out of it. 'Yes, here we are . . . and Emilia, I see you did well with your new patient! Emilia here saved my life for sure, Mr Kenny . . . you're in good hands.'

'Yes, unfortunately she's engaged to marry that poor printer . . . no hope for us Kenny boys!' Eddie said, with a forced laugh.

Cal had been thinking about her all night, after everyone had pulled out of Blood Creek, except Cy and Lizzie, who were there at that moment, probably giving Sedge a proper burial and a prayer, he thought to himself.

'Well, my brother's goin' nowhere. Doctor's orders. He was no more than a hair's breadth from leaving this room in a box,' Jake said.

A while later, when the different feeling around the town meant that good things would happen – such as Gibbs and Charlie running the newspaper again, and the Heath Hotel staying with the Heath name – Cal and Matt rested up in the room outside Kenny's sick-room and they chewed the fat over their future, with a bottle of brandy offered to them from Doc Heath's medicine supplies.

'For me, Cal,' Matt explained, 'I'm in a mood to work on my own. The Pinkerton way is a mite too busy with orders . . . like the army agin. That Lerade, he's a hard taskmaster, and he worries like an old woman!'

'You don't mean bounty-hunting, surely?' Cal asked, lazily.

'If it earns, then yes. I'll always have the itch to keep movin', and I got things to forget. The past never leaves off plaguing a man, Cal. Mind, I've had more than my fill of gunfire just now. If I was a mite younger I could ride shotgun on a stage.'

'No. You're like me, Matt Calero. . . restless. You can't resist lookin' out there at that horizon, can you?'

'You neither, Cal Roney. What are you fixin' to do now?'

Cal took a swig of the brandy and wiped his mouth. He had felt the confusion of a hundred different thoughts and feelings running around his head ever since Matt had shot dead Jim Kenny, and the future was closing down again, when Emilia was spoken for. For a few days at least, he had enjoyed the dream of being that strange thing, a husband, looking after that other, stranger thing, a wife. Now it was all gone, that settling down feeling. The frontier offer its endless opportunities to him yet again.

'Matt, you know, I think I'll ride on north after we get these murderin' swine locked up in Laramie.'

'North? Indian country?'

'Maybe. But you know, the Sioux and their kin have done some sensible decidin' in life . . . homes you can move around with, and beef on the next plain.'

'Maybe you could use a partner?' Matt asked, though Cal could not gauge whether he was serious or not. He pondered for a moment, looked down at the table, and then said, 'You know, my friend, you're the closest thing to a brother I ever had, and two guns are better than one if a man's in a tight spot. But. . . .'

'But you're too mule-headed to play along with another, and you're riding alone, right?'

'Right. Thick in the head, ain't I?'

'Sometimes the lone steer gets more chow!' Matt said, and the humour of it filled his head so much he had to belly-laugh, and the humour spread. 'Anyway, I suffer from the same thickness up here . . . no sense at all. . . .' He tapped his skull playfully.

'Well, you don't owe me nothin', and you know, I have no memory of anything that happened once, or might have happened, or probably didn't happen, in a certain battle.' Cal was looking up at the ceiling as he said this, as if it was all going to be anonymous.

They enjoyed a laugh, but later that day, when both Kenny brothers were locked into the sickroom and Ben Stile sat on guard, the Pinkerton men were assigned to watch the road. Neither Ben nor anybody else in Long Corral trusted the Double T cowhands. They could come riding in at any time and bust out their bosses by force.

'If they come ridin' hard, you take the first man . . . and I'll side-winder myself along this walkway and cover you, brother . . .' Matt said, looking for a response.

'Brother . . . I like that. I might ride alone, but you're a brother more than kin.' Cal was aware that what had once been something that gave his friend a sense of shame was now rubbed out forever, like a hard lesson on the board at school, when teacher called home-time.

Cal had another long silence to stand: another long wait, with a job to do, and his mind had hours and hours to churn around what might happen in the coming time. Somehow, he thought – and you could call it fate if you wanted to – he was meant to ride alone, with that little shiver of healthy fear of the unknown ahead, and the mistakes of the past well behind.